Introduction

On the docket today

- Humanity -

The Charge

High Treason

Copyright © 2011 by Mark A. Hornbeck

Dedication

First and foremost, I dedicate this book to my Lord and Savior, Jesus Christ, who in His infinite mercy reached down and grasped me from the clutches of Satan and his new age philosophy, and caused me to remember the loving God of my youth as taught by my godly parents.

Secondly, I dedicate this book to my loving wife, Bonnie, who patiently bore long months acting either as my sounding board or enduring my absence behind my computer screen and Bible. It could not have been done without her encouragement and support.

Finally, I dedicate this book to the men and women who, through earnest prayer, fasting, and the deep study of God's word, founded the SDA Church. These individuals sacrificed all on the altar of truth. With God's infinite guidance and the testimony of Jesus through His prophetic gift, they established the sound doctrinal pillars of truth of His final remnant church, of whom I am blessed to be a member.

Special Thanks

In a special way I would like to express my heartfelt appreciation to Rachel Weeks who spent countless hours taking a very rough draft and making it presentable. Without her hard work and expertise this book could not have been possible.

Table of Contents

1. Universe of Light ……….. Pg. 9
2. Fall into Darkness ……… Pg. 19
3. Revelations of Light …… Pg. 34
4. God is One……………..….. Pg. 46
5. Source of Confusion …… Pg. 65
6. War in the Wilderness ….. Pg. 106
7. Victory in the Garden …... Pg. 118
8. Three Unclean Spirits …… Pg. 127
9. Revelations of the Cross in the Sanctuary

5 Parts
1. The North ……………..…. Pg. 156
2. The South ……………….. Pg. 170
3. The East ………………….. Pg. 184
4. The West ………………….. Pg. 194
5. The Ark of the Covenant … Pg. 202

Final Chapter
10. Not by Might Nor by Power Pg. 208

Preface

As we face the final events of this earth's history, we find that attacks are bearing down upon us, His remnant people, at an alarming rate. As the church is besieged by attacks, from without and within, we find that many lose faith and fall by the wayside. Many expect absolute perfection from the church. When confronted by its enfeebled mistakes, they fall off the path and then attack the church with the same passion and zeal they once held for it. Forgotten are the words: "**During ages of spiritual darkness the church of God has been as a city set on a hill. From age to age, through successive generations, the pure doctrines of heaven have been unfolding within its borders. Enfeebled and defective as it may appear, the church is the one object upon which God bestows in a special sense His supreme regard. It is the theater of His grace, in which He delights to reveal His power to transform hearts.**" AA 12

Here, in the last moments of earth's history, we are shown that God's church will be enfeebled and have some imperfections that will have to be addressed by God. We are even told that at the end of time the church would face a terrible apostasy that would shake it to its very foundations. "**The Omega (of apostasies) would follow in a little while. I tremble for our people. <u>These beautiful representations (of this apostasy) are</u>**

similar to the temptation that the enemy brought to Adam and Eve in Eden." 1SAT 341

This apostasy would be so profound and powerful by its very nature that the church would even appear about to fall. "**The church may appear as about to fall, but it does not fall. It remains, while the sinners in Zion will be sifted out--the chaff separated from the precious wheat. This is a terrible ordeal, but nevertheless it must take place.** 2SM 380

This book addresses the high treason of mankind and the provision for salvation provided by God through Jesus Christ our Lord. We will examine the attacks by Satan who seeks to prevent this gift of salvation from being realized by God's final remnant church. We will examine the inroads of deception that have infiltrated this final movement of God.

However, one should not see this book's illumination of Satan's attacks, in the form of doctrines and teachings, as an attack on God's final remnant church or its people. This book and its author totally rejects any notion that these attacks within the church signify that the church has fallen or has become Babylon, as many who have fallen by the wayside try to teach or proclaim. This work is not a call to leave the church but just the opposite. It is a call for God's remnant to stand and fortify the walls of Zion.

It is because the shaking must come, as revealed by the prophet, and because it will be a terrible ordeal for God's people that this book is written. It is to reveal the arrows of error fired into our midst and to shine light on the shield of truth as provided by God for His people. It is to arm God's remnant with the truth of Jesus and His Father, so that we may stand in the great trial before us that these pages have been penned.

Many will find that some doctrines that they have held as truth will not stand the test of the Bible as they thought. Others will find, although they have a certain understanding of truths presented in the word, that there is a deeper truth that as yet they have not seen or understood. Many will find the disturbing truth that Satan, over time and generations, has attacked the fundamental foundational pillars of our faith as lain down by God through the pioneers of our church. They will see that some of these fundamental truths have been changed or rejected by many, from laymen to leaders, within the remnant church. We are in trouble and the night is nearly past. The day is about to dawn.

It is the straight testimony of these truths that many will not accept, and the rebellion against this straight testimony will bring about the great shaking that is coming upon us. "**I asked the meaning of the shaking I had seen, and was shown that it would be caused by the straight testimony called forth by the counsel of the True Witness to the Laodiceans. This will have its effect upon the heart of the receiver, and will lead him to exalt the standard and pour forth the straight truth. Some will not bear this straight** testimony. They will rise up against it, and this is what will cause a shaking among God's people.

I saw that the testimony of the True Witness has not been half heeded. The solemn testimony upon which the destiny of the church hangs has been lightly esteemed, if not entirely disregarded. This testimony must work deep repentance; all who truly receive it will obey it, and be purified. CET 176

"Son of man, I have made thee a watchman unto the house of Israel: therefore hear the word at my mouth, and give them warning from me." (Ezekiel 3:17) As a watchman on the wall of Zion I raise the alarm to you now. **Awake** for the enemy is upon us.

Chapter 1
Universe of Light

"*The heavens declare the glory of God; and the firmament sheweth his handywork.*" (Psalm 19:1) Throughout the universe, all of creation resonated with a single peaceful harmony of existence. Since the beginning of time, when the Creator spoke the universe into existence, it had always been so for: "*Thus saith God the LORD, he that created the heavens, and stretched them out.*" (Isaiah 42:5) Throughout the depths of time, its inhabitants looked into the heavens and marveled at the magnificence of the Divine. There was no limit to His power, and as all creation looked upon His works, they cried: "*Alleluia: for the Lord God omnipotent reigneth.*" (Revelation 19:6)

As we look back into time past, out into the vast universe, we look back past the beginning of the great cosmic civil war and deep into the ancient depths of time. We see approximately 100 billion galaxies with each hosting as many as 100 billion to even a trillion stars. Yet, in spite of their vast numbers, each star is guided unerringly in its divinely oriented path. "*Lift up your eyes on high, and behold who hath created these things, that bringeth out their host by number: he calleth them all by names by the greatness of his might, for that he is strong in power; not one faileth.*" (Isaiah 40:26) "*That they may see, and know, and consider, and understand together, that the hand of the LORD hath done this, and the Holy One of Israel hath created it."* (Isaiah 41:20) *"Who is this King of glory? The LORD of hosts, he is the King of glory"* (Psalm 24:10).

All of creation existed in joy and peace under this benevolent ruler. By the God of creation, all had been created under the expressed law of His Father's love. As all looked upon the creation of God: *"the morning stars sang together, and all the sons of God shouted for joy."* (Job 38:7) They could see the manifestation of God's love in all that was created for: *"Is not God in the height of heaven? and behold the height of the stars, how high they are!"* (Job 22:12)

At the center of the universe lay the crowned jewel of creation, the capital city of the Ancient of Days. Ruling heaven and all this universe was God the Father and His beloved Son, Michael. Together, they were surrounded by a multitude of angels whom they loved and who loved them in return. Together, they ruled in love and power over the universe in all its dazzling glory and beauty. Those who visited heaven were *"come unto mount Sion and unto the city of the living God, the heavenly Jerusalem, and to an innumerable company of angels."* (Hebrews 12:22)

The 19th century author and theologian Ellen White described it this way. **"The Sovereign of the universe was not alone in His work of beneficence. He had an associate--a co-worker who could appreciate His purposes, and could share His joy in giving** happiness to created beings. "*In the beginning was the Word, and the Word was with God, and the Word was God. The same was in the beginning with God.*" John 1:1, 2.

Christ, the Word, the only begotten of God, was one with the eternal Father--one in nature, in character, in purpose--<u>the only being</u> that could enter into all the counsels and purposes of God. "*His name shall be called Wonderful, Counselor, The mighty God, The everlasting Father, The Prince of Peace.*" Isaiah 9:6. His "*goings forth have been from of old, from everlasting.*" Micah 5:2. And the Son of God declares concerning Himself: "*The Lord possessed Me in the beginning of His way, before His works of old. I was set up from everlasting. . . . When He appointed the foundations of the earth: then I was by Him, as one brought up with Him: and I was daily His delight, rejoicing always before Him.*" Proverbs 8:22-30.

The Father wrought by His Son in the creation of all heavenly beings. "*By Him were all things created, . . . whether they be thrones, or dominions, or principalities, or powers: all things were created by Him, and for Him.*" Colossians 1:16. Angels are God's ministers, radiant with the light ever flowing from His presence and speeding on rapid wing to execute His will. But the Son, the anointed of God, the *"express image of His person," "the brightness of His glory," "upholding all things by the word of His power,"* holds supremacy over them all. Hebrews 1:3. "*A glorious high throne from the beginning,"* was the place of His sanctuary (Jeremiah 17:12); *"a scepter of righteousness,"* the scepter of His kingdom. Hebrews 1:8. *"Honor and majesty are before Him: strength and beauty are in His sanctuary."* Psalm 96:6. *"Mercy and truth go before His face".* Psalm 89:14.

The law of love being the foundation of the government of God, the happiness of all intelligent beings depends upon their perfect accord with its great principles of righteousness. God desires from all His creatures the service of love--service that springs from an appreciation of His character. He takes no pleasure in a forced obedience; and to all He grants freedom of will, that they may render Him voluntary service.

So long as all created beings acknowledged the allegiance of love, there was perfect harmony throughout the universe of God. It was the joy of the heavenly host to fulfill the purpose of their Creator. They delighted in reflecting His glory and showing forth His praise. And while love to God was supreme, love for one another was confiding and unselfish. There was no note of discord to mar the celestial harmonies." PP 34-35

Through the eons of time, all of creation basked in the rays of infinite divine love. With each new work of creation, the universe was ever expanding into new depths of wonder and beauty. It was a paradise beyond description with no trace of evil to tarnish its existence. Worlds of beauty, far surpassing the imaginations of man, showed forth in splendor and majesty as the Son worked in artistic joy and love, ever adding to its boundless variety and beauty. Powerful telescopes, even today, are able to peer back across the light years of space and time and see glimpses of the incredible beauty wrought by His mighty hand.

The Father's deep and matchless love for His Son was also expressed towards all of His creation. It pleased Him for Michael to be loved and exalted. E. J. Waggoner expressed it well in his book <u>CHRIST AND HIS RIGHTEOUSNESS</u>. He states that there was: **"not a thing in the universe that Christ did not create. He made everything in heaven and everything on earth. He made everything that can be seen and everything that cannot be seen--the thrones and dominions and the principalities and the powers in heaven, all depend upon Him for existence. And as He is before all things and their Creator, so by Him do all things consist or hold together. This is equivalent to what is said in Heb. 1:3, that He upholds all things by the word of His power. It was by a word that the heavens were made, and that same word holds them in their place and preserves them from destruction.**

We cannot possibly omit in this connection Isa. 40:25, 26: "*To whom then will ye liken me, or shall I be equal? saith the Holy One. Lift up your eyes on high and behold who hath created these things, that bringeth out their host by number; he calleth them all by names by the greatness of his might, for that he is strong in power; not one faileth."* Or, as the Jewish translation more forcibly renders it, *"from him, who is great in might, and strong in power, not one escapeth."* That Christ is the Holy One who thus calls the host of heaven by name and holds them in their place is evident from other portions of the same chapter. He is the One before whom it was said, *"Prepare ye the way of the Lord, make straight in the desert a highway for our God."* He is the One who comes with a strong hand, having His reward with Him; the One who, like a shepherd, feeds His flock, carrying the lambs in His bosom.

One more statement concerning Christ as Creator must suffice. It is the testimony of the Father Himself. In the first chapter of Hebrews, we read that God has spoken to us by His Son; that He said of Him, *"Let all the angels of God worship him"* that of the angels He saith, *"Who maketh his angels spirits, and His ministers a flame of fire,"* but that He says to the Son, *"Thy throne, O God, is forever and ever; a scepter of righteousness is the scepter of Thy kingdom."* And God says further, *"Thou, Lord, in the beginning hast laid the foundation of the earth, and the heavens are the works of thine hands."* Heb. 1:8-10. Here we find the Father addressing the Son as God, and saying to Him, Thou hast laid the foundations of the earth, and the heavens are the work of Thy hands. When the Father Himself gives this honor to the Son, what is man, that he should withhold it? With this we may well leave the direct testimony concerning the Divinity of Christ and the fact that He is the Creator of all things.

A word of caution may be necessary here. Let no one imagine that we would exalt Christ at the expense of the Father or would ignore the Father. That cannot be, for their interests are one. We honor the Father in honoring the Son. We are mindful of Paul's words, that "*to us there is but one God, the Father, of whom are all things, and we in him; and one Lord Jesus Christ, by whom are all things, and we by him*" (1 Cor. 8:6); just as we have already quoted, that it was by Him that God made the worlds. All things proceed ultimately from God, the Father; even Christ Himself proceeded and came forth from the Father, but it has pleased the Father that in Him should all fullness dwell, and that He should be the direct, immediate Agent in every act of creation. Our object in this investigation is to set forth Christ's rightful position of equality with the Father, in order that His power to redeem may be the better appreciated." CR Chapter 4

Lest there be confusion on the relationship of the Father and Son, Waggoner continues on stating: **'The Scriptures declare that Christ is "*the only begotten son of God*." He is begotten, not created. As to when He was begotten, it is not for us to inquire, nor could our minds grasp it if we were told. The prophet Micah tells us all that we can know about it in these words, "*But thou, Bethlehem Ephratah, though thou be little among the thousands of Judah, yet out of thee shall He come* *forth unto Me that is to be ruler in Israel; whose goings forth have been from of old, from the days of eternity."* Micah 5:2, margin. There was a time when Christ proceeded forth and came from God, from the bosom of the Father (John 8:42; 1:18), but that time was so far back in the days of eternity that to finite comprehension it is practically without beginning." CR Chapter 5

Indeed this relationship was older than the universe itself, for it was through Michael that all creation existed. From the smallest atom to the largest galaxy, all expressed the Creator's power and love. Finally, a time came when Michael turned His face toward our small corner of the universe and by the word of His mouth and the power innate within Himself created this untainted world, its life, and finally mankind in His image.

As we in turn looked into the heavens and into His mighty vast creation, it led us to ask: *"When I consider thy heavens, the work of thy fingers, the moon and the stars, which thou hast ordained, what is man, that thou art mindful of him, and the son of man, that thou visitest him? For thou hast made him a little lower than the angels, and hast crowned him with glory and honour."* (Psalm 8:4-6) Placed in a garden of unsurpassed beauty, man joined the cosmic community of creation in glorifying, by praise and worship, his loving Creator.

Yet, even as God was planning the creation of man, all this happiness was to come to an abrupt halt. This unmarred universe full of perfection fell into a stupendous crisis as the unthinkable crept into existence. Indeed, it took root in the very heart of heaven itself as an angel of high order and magnificence, without provocation, committed high treason against the most high God. Civil war broke out as the very nature of God, His relationship to His Son, Michael, and His immutable law of love came under fire. The universe looked on in horror as the colossal conflict finally erupted into battle. Lucifer, guilty of high treason against the government of heaven, convinced a full third of the heavenly angels to rebel with him and together they fought against Michael and His angels. How long this battle of revolt lasted we are not told, but Lucifer and his angels did not prevail.

"And there was war in heaven: Michael and his angels fought against the dragon; and the dragon fought and his angels, And prevailed not; neither was their place found any more in heaven. And the great dragon was cast out, that old serpent, called the Devil, and Satan, which deceiveth the whole world: he was cast out into the earth, and his angels were cast out with him." (Revelation 12:7-9) Overthrown, they were cast from heaven in disgrace, and the greatest conflict of all time was underway.

It is to this story and how man joined in that rebellion that we will now look. We are involved in the most tragic story of mutiny against the most high God, and in the amazing story of what our fate will be in the final events of this war. We did not stay loyal to our rightful Sovereign. Instead, like Lucifer's angels, we joined in that dreadful rebellion. Like them, we found ourselves in shame standing before the highest courts having been charged, tried, and found guilty of high treason against our Creator and His Father, the most high God! The Sentence, Death!

Chapter 2
The Fall into Darkness

It had been some time since Michael had gone into the presence of God. They were having a serious conference of some type and Lucifer wondered what it was all about. Many times he had been included in Michael's plans but never in the inner counsels with God. This privilege had only been given to God's Son, Michael. As he waited he began to wonder why he could not be included in these counsels. Why was God only allowing Michael into His plans?

Ellen White wrote: "**The Sovereign of the universe was not alone in His work of beneficence. He had an associate--a co-worker who could appreciate His purposes, and could share His joy in giving happiness to created beings.** *"In the beginning was the Word, and the Word was with God, and the Word was God. The same was in the beginning with God."* **John 1:1-2. Christ, the Word, the only begotten of God, was one with the eternal Father--one in nature, in character, in purpose--<u>the only being that could enter into all the counsels and purposes of God</u>.** " PP 33

As Lucifer stood watch, Michael finally came out from the presence of the Father, out from the infinite brightness that enshrouded Him. With a loving smile Michael greeted him. Lucifer, in loving admiration, smiled back at his Creator. Michael had created him and exalted him, allowing him to be the covering cherub, and it was Lucifer's privilege to be the highest ranking angel in heaven. In many of the operations of heaven, he had been honored to be included. With his high rank, he had been given the highest honor among the angels and was allowed to walk where few had gone. God, speaking of him through His prophet Ezekiel, stated: *"Thou art the anointed cherub that covereth; and I have set thee so: thou wast upon the holy mountain of God; thou hast walked up and down in the midst of the stones of fire."* (Ezekiel 28:14)

Because of his brightness from being in the presence of God and because of his own beauty, Lucifer was admired and loved by the heavenly angels.

As Michael went out among the angels, they all in loving admiration worshiped Him as they always had done. This time, as Lucifer watched Michael, a strange new emotion stirred within him. Why shouldn't he be admired <u>and</u> worshipped like Michael? Why should worship belong only to Michael and the Father? Was not he also beautiful and powerful? Even God could see this.

"Thus saith the Lord God; Thou sealest up the sum, full of wisdom, and perfect in beauty. Thou hast been in Eden the garden of God; every precious stone was thy covering. . . . Thou art the anointed cherub that covereth; and I have set thee so: thou wast upon the holy mountain of God; thou hast walked up and down in the midst of the stones of fire. Thou wast perfect in thy ways

from the day that thou wast created, till iniquity was found in thee." (Ezekiel 28:12-15)

At first Lucifer put the thought aside and did not give it further contemplation, but as time went by he began to dwell more and more on his beauty. Each time he observed the angels worshipping Michael, jealousy stirred within him, and he began to covet that worship desiring it for himself. After all, what was this distinction between being born of the Father versus being created by the Father? Shouldn't he also be considered a true son of the Father?

In speaking of this Ellen White wrote: **"Little by little Lucifer came to indulge the desire for self-exaltation. The Scripture says, "*Thine heart was lifted up because of thy beauty, thou hast corrupted thy wisdom by reason of thy brightness.*" Ezekiel 28:17. "*Thou hast said in thine heart, . . . I will exalt my throne above the stars of God. . . . I will be like the Most High.*" Isaiah 14:13, 14. Though all his glory was from God, this mighty angel came to regard it as pertaining to himself. Not content with his position, though honored above the heavenly host, he ventured to covet homage due alone to the Creator. Instead of seeking to make God supreme in the affections and allegiance of all created beings, it was his endeavor to secure their service and loyalty to himself. And coveting the <u>glory with which the infinite Father had invested His Son</u>, this prince of angels aspired to power that was the prerogative of Christ alone."** PP 35

Finally, Lucifer decided that he was being wronged by God the Father in denying him the same prerogatives that the Father gave to Michael. He came to believe that God's law, that required worship of the Father and His Son only, was selfish and unjust. He began to see this as a sign of evil in the heart and nature of God. He felt that it was not a law of love, but that it was rooted in selfishness. Finally, he began to quietly express his views to other angels. The fact that he had been given the highest position among the angels was to Lucifer not enough.

"The high honors conferred upon Lucifer were not appreciated as God's special gift, and therefore, called forth no gratitude to his Creator. He gloried in his brightness and exaltation and aspired to be equal with God. He was beloved and reverenced by the heavenly host, angels delighted to execute his commands, and he was clothed with wisdom and glory above them all. Yet the Son of God was exalted above him, as one in power and authority with the Father. He shared the Father's counsels, while Lucifer did not thus enter into the purposes of God. "Why," questioned this mighty angel, "should Christ have the supremacy? Why is He honored above Lucifer?

Leaving his place in the immediate presence of the Father, Lucifer went forth to diffuse the spirit of discontent among the angels. He worked with mysterious secrecy, and for a time concealed his real purpose under an appearance of reverence for God. He began to insinuate doubts concerning the laws that governed heavenly beings, intimating that though laws might be necessary for the inhabitants of the worlds, angels, being more exalted, needed no such restraint, for their own wisdom was a sufficient guide. They were not beings that could bring dishonor to God; all their thoughts were holy; it was no more possible for them than for God Himself to err. The exaltation of the Son of God as equal with the Father was represented as an injustice to Lucifer, who, it was claimed, was also entitled to reverence and honor. If this prince of angels could but attain to his true, exalted position, great good would accrue to the entire host of heaven; for it was his object to secure freedom for all. But now even the liberty which they had hitherto enjoyed was at an end; for an absolute Ruler had been appointed them, and to His authority all must pay homage. Such were the subtle deceptions that through the wiles of Lucifer were fast obtaining in the heavenly courts.

There had been no change in the position or authority of Christ. Lucifer's envy and misrepresentation and his claims to equality with Christ had made necessary a statement of the true position of the Son of God; but this had been the same from the beginning. Many of the angels were, however, blinded by Lucifer's deceptions." PP 36-38

Seeing where Lucifer was headed, Michael came to him and in compassion showed him where this rebellious path was leading. He loved Lucifer deeply and hoped to reason with him. In infinite love and pity He laid out how if God's law was broken that it would plummet Lucifer and any of his followers into an abyss of unhappiness, misery, sorrow, ruin and finally death. It was still not too late, if only he would turn from this path and return to the harmonious love of his Creator. Rather than listen to Michael, Lucifer only misinterpreted everything He said.

"A compassionate Creator, in yearning pity for Lucifer and his followers, was seeking to draw them back from the abyss of ruin into which they were about to plunge. But His mercy was misinterpreted. Lucifer pointed to the long-suffering of God as an evidence of his own superiority, an indication that the King of the universe would yet accede to his terms. If the angels would stand firmly with him, he declared, they could yet gain all that they desired. He persistently defended his own course, and fully committed himself to the great controversy against his Maker. Thus it was that Lucifer, "the light bearer," the sharer of God's glory, the attendant of His throne, by transgression became Satan, "the adversary" of God and holy beings and the destroyer of those whom Heaven had committed to his guidance and guardianship." PP 39-40

As the rebellion progressed, Lucifer began to propagate a three part lie that spread among the angels. He implied, first, that angels did not need Michael, the Son of God, and implied that they could exist and live without this slavery or servitude to the unfair and selfish leader. He presented that they themselves should also be considered God's sons. God was playing favorites with Michael and was consequently wronging them as well.

Secondly, Lucifer said that angels could by their own powers and devices enlighten themselves into a higher plane of existence that was rightfully theirs and was within their innate abilities.

Finally, Lucifer convinced them that, like Michael, they could be gods having the same knowledge and power. This after all, he pressed, is what God was keeping from them.

Events in heaven finally came to the place where Michael and His Father could allow it to go no further. Through Lucifer's corrupting subterfuge, a full third of the angels had joined in the rebellion. All of God's attempts to reason with them had failed. In full rebellion, Lucifer declared open revolt against God and war broke out in heaven.

Lucifer in his pride thought to actually fight against God. *"For thou hast said in thine heart, I will ascend into heaven, I will exalt my throne above the stars of God: I will sit also upon the mount of the congregation, in the sides of the north: I will ascend above the heights of the clouds; I will be like the most High."* (Isaiah 14:13-14) *"And there was war in heaven: Michael and his angels fought against the dragon; and the dragon fought and his angels, And prevailed not;*

neither was their place found any more in heaven. And the great dragon was cast out, that old serpent, called the Devil, and Satan ... he was cast out into the earth, and his angels were cast out with him." (Revelation 12:7)

The Father did not destroy Lucifer and his followers immediately. In His wisdom, He knew that the accusations against His character, His Son, and the lies concerning His law of love, had raised questions that would have to be answered. Only with love and obedience, given within the boundaries of freedom of choice, could the charges be met and shown to be false. Among the unfallen worlds, the issue of the nature of the Father and His Son, and their law of love and obedience, must be laid out. In light of the truth, each world must be given the freedom of choice to choose their allegiance.

Among these unfallen worlds was a new world that had just been created. Earth, in all its new beauty, was now to be given the same freedom to choose. I will not go into all the details of humanity's test and fall at this point. We all know the story. Adam and Eve did not believe God. By eating of the tree of knowledge of good and evil, mankind was plunged into that great rebellion against God.

An evaluation here of what was offered to our fallen parents is of great importance. In heaven, Lucifer wanted to be like God. He thought that he could be like the Most High. He believed that created beings did not need to worship God's Son and that like Michael they could be as God. Thus, in his first lies to our parents, he presented the same philosophy. He offered the same idea that they could be free of God's selfish demands and even be like God. He presented an idea that by being free of God's law and His Son they could reach a higher state of existence.

"And the serpent [Satan] said unto the woman, Ye shall not surely die: for God doth know that in the day ye eat thereof, then your eyes shall be opened, and ye shall be as gods, knowing good and evil." By partaking of this tree, he declared, they would attain to a more exalted sphere of existence and enter a broader field of knowledge … When she [Eve] "saw that the tree was good for food, and that it was pleasant to the eyes, and a tree to be desired to make one wise, she took of the fruit thereof, and did eat." It was grateful to the taste, and as she ate, she seemed to feel a vivifying power, and imagined herself entering upon a higher state of existence … After his transgression Adam at first imagined himself entering upon a higher state of existence." PP 54-55

Such has been Satan's work from the days of Adam to the present, and he has pursued it unfortunately with great success. For over six thousand years Satan has perfected and used these three lies to keep mankind under his subjugation and domain.

We will see later in this book that believing God and not falling for Satan's three lies is still the great test for mankind. It was involved in the alpha of apostasies that would attack God's developing remnant church near the end of time. It will be at the heart of Lucifer's final attack. It will be the root of the last great omega of apostasies in God's remnant church right before Christ's second coming.

With Adams fall, what would God do now that the rebellion was spreading? Would He instantly destroy man? **"With intense interest the unfallen worlds had watched to see Jehovah arise, and sweep away the inhabitants of the earth. And if God should do this, Satan was ready to carry out his plan for securing to himself the allegiance of heavenly beings. He had declared that the principles of God's government make forgiveness impossible. Had the world been destroyed, he would have claimed that his accusations were proved true. He was ready to cast blame upon God, and to spread his rebellion to the worlds above."** DA 31

What God would do next would very likely decide the fate of the entire universe. The omnipotent power of God could not be used to wipe out sin through power alone without throwing the whole universe into anarchy. Ironically, the answer lay in the very character of God that Lucifer was attacking. It lay at the heart of God's law of love. What God would do next would become the most amazing act that has ever occurred and will never again be matched throughout the eons of time.

Ellen White described it best when she wrote: **"The fall of man filled all heaven with sorrow. The** world that God had made was blighted with the curse of sin and inhabited by beings doomed to misery and death. There appeared no escape for those who had transgressed the law. Angels ceased their songs of praise. Throughout the heavenly courts there was mourning for the ruin that sin had wrought.

The Son of God, heaven's glorious Commander, was touched with pity for the fallen race. His heart was moved with infinite compassion as the woes of the lost world rose up before Him. But divine love had conceived a plan whereby man might be redeemed. The broken law of God demanded the life of the sinner. In all the universe there was but one who could, in behalf of man, satisfy its claims. Since the divine law is as sacred as God Himself, only one equal with God could make atonement for its transgression. None but Christ could redeem fallen man from the curse of the law and bring him again into harmony with Heaven. Christ would take upon Himself the guilt and shame of sin--sin so offensive to a holy God that it must separate the Father and His Son. Christ would reach to the depths of misery to rescue the ruined race.

Before the Father He pleaded in the sinner's behalf, while the host of heaven awaited the result with an intensity of interest that words cannot express. Long continued was that mysterious communing--"the counsel of peace" (Zechariah 6:13) for the fallen sons of men. The plan of salvation had been laid before the creation of the earth; for Christ is "the Lamb slain from the foundation of the world" (Revelation 13:8); yet it was a struggle, even with the King of the universe, to yield up His Son to die for the guilty race. But "God so loved the world, that He gave His only-begotten Son, that whosoever believeth in Him should not perish, but have everlasting life." John 3:16. Oh, the mystery of redemption! The love of God for a world that did not love Him! Who can know the depths of that love which "passeth knowledge"? Through endless ages immortal minds, seeking to comprehend the mystery of that incomprehensible love, will wonder and adore.

God was to be manifest in Christ, "reconciling the world unto Himself." 2 Corinthians 5:19. Man had become so degraded by sin that it was impossible for him, in himself, to come into harmony with Him whose nature is purity and goodness. But Christ, after having redeemed man from the condemnation of the law, could impart divine power to unite with human effort. Thus by repentance toward God and faith in Christ the fallen children of Adam might once more become "sons of God." 1 John 3:2.

The plan by which alone man's salvation could be secured, involved all heaven in its infinite sacrifice. The angels could not rejoice as Christ opened before them the plan of redemption, for they saw that man's salvation must cost their loved Commander unutterable woe. In grief and wonder they listened to His words as He told them how He must descend from heaven's purity and peace, its joy and glory and immortal life, and come in contact with the degradation of earth, to endure its sorrow, shame, and death. He was to stand between the sinner and the penalty of sin; yet few would receive Him as the Son of God. He would leave His high position as the Majesty of heaven, appear upon earth and humble Himself as a man, and by His own experience become acquainted with the sorrows and temptations which man would have to endure. All this would be necessary in order that He might be able to succor them that should be tempted. Hebrews 2:18. When His mission as a teacher should be ended, He must be delivered into the hands of wicked men and be subjected to every insult and torture that Satan could inspire them to inflict. He must die the cruelest of deaths, lifted up between the heavens and the earth as a guilty sinner. He must pass long hours of agony so terrible that angels could not look upon it, but would veil their faces from the sight. He must endure anguish of soul, the hiding of His Father's face, while the guilt of transgression--the weight of the sins of the whole world--should be upon Him." PP 63-64

Yes, Michael was to come and reveal the character of the Father and His law of love and, at the same time, redeem our fallen race. Yes, we were found guilty of high treason, and yes, death would be the penalty. But the Father would pay the price with the life of His only Son. This would not only work for the salvation of man but would finally reveal in a full revelation the nature of God and His amazing law of love. It is to this nature we will now turn.

Satan had from the outset tried to malign God's nature and even today still tries to hide it in a shroud of mystery. Many false doctrines have been spawned by Satan in order to frame God in a false light. There are very few subjects that have sparked more debate and confusion among Christians and theologians today than that of the nature of God. Who or what is God? Is it a divine trilogy of beings, as Catholicism and much of Protestantism teach, or only one God, as many Jews believe? If, indeed, there are three Gods, how does the Christian separate himself from the many pagan polytheistic religions that dominate much of the world?

There seems to be no end of theories concerning not only who or what God is but also on how much about our Divine Creator we can understand. Is it a mystery beyond our ability to comprehend? Has God enshrouded Himself in a cloud of inviolable enigma, a veil of which no one can ever hope to look beyond? Is God so incredibly powerful and immense that even our wildest and most intensive endeavors of fathoming Him are impotent and fall utterly in the realm of complete ignorance and hopelessness? Or has God chosen to reveal Himself to us? If He has, then how much has He revealed? Is He spirit or does He have substance like you and me? What is the Spirit of God? What is this mysterious part of what some refer to as the Godhead?

Is it a separate entity from the Father, having thoughts and a consciousness of its own individuality?

What of the Son of God? Why is He called the Son of God? What is His relationship to the Father? These and other questions about God, and the answers to them, have divided not only one denomination from another but has even been the source of rifts that occur between members within denominations and their individual churches.

Beliefs on these subjects are usually deep seated and staunchly defended, even in the face of overwhelming evidence against them. It is a fact that more wars and atrocities have been committed in the name of God and religion than for all other reasons combined. But does God intend us to be in the dark concerning Himself, or is it the work of another power that would seek to keep God a mystery to us?

Has God been a mystery to us or did God reveal Himself to our founding church fathers? Through these founders and through the prophetic gift, did He establish a firm foundation for His church in doctrines that reveals Himself to us? If He did, then has Satan been busy undermining these truths? We must examine these questions and find the answers as we explore deeper into the revelations of God.

Chapter 3
Revelations of Light

"And this is life eternal, that they might know thee the only true God, and Jesus Christ, whom thou hast sent". The words of Christ in John 17:3 echo to our time. They address the one basic question we must answer before we proceed. Is God a mystery beyond our ability to understand? How much does God want us to understand about Him? What does it mean to **know** Him? This is a vital question and must be answered. If He desires to be a distant and inconceivable God, one who is unfathomable and above our reckoning, then we truly should not seek to delve into forbidden doctrines.

There are many who believe that God is too vast for us to understand. Many feel that seeking to understand God is wrong and even blasphemous. To them, God is a mystery, a mystical unity of a divine triune, yet singular holy being that pervades all of creation. They view Him as one who wants to remain a mystery to His creation. We are viewed as being too small and insignificant to need to understand God. We must accept Him knowing little about Him. Job 11:7-9 seems to reaffirm this: *"Canst thou by searching find out God? canst thou find out the Almighty unto perfection? It is as high as heaven; what canst thou do? deeper than hell; what canst thou know? The measure thereof is longer than the earth, and broader than the sea."* This text would seem to suggest that we cannot by searching find God. Indeed, it was written as a scold for one who was trying to understand God. For the surface reader this supports the "God is a Mystery" theory.

Yet, this text is a trap for those who do not read the context in which it was written. This text was the words of Job's friend, Zophar, the Naamathite. It was part of his wicked counsel to Job. Job held a different view, as was seen in part of his answer to his friends. He said: *"I know that my redeemer liveth, and that he shall stand at the latter day upon the earth… Yet in my flesh shall I see God:"* God later addressed these two different views. In Job 42:7-8 we read: *"The LORD said to Eliphaz the Temanite, My wrath is kindled against thee, and against thy two friends: for ye have not spoken of me the thing that is right, as my servant Job hath… him will I accept: lest I deal with you after your folly, in that ye have not spoken of me the thing which is right, like my servant Job."*

God revealed that these words of Zophar were not inspired nor did they represent God's will for man. Although Job was not meant to fully understand all of God's purposes, nor the depth of His power and wisdom, he was still to know and understand who God was.

Christ's words reveal this in John 17. He reveals that life eternal is available to those who know the only true God. Let's explore this further. In Jeremiah 10 we read, *"...the LORD is the true God, he is the living God, and an everlasting king…..Thus shall ye say unto them, The gods that have not made the heavens and the earth, even they shall perish from the earth, and from under these heavens. He hath made the earth by his power, he hath established the world by his wisdom, and hath stretched out the heavens by his discretion."* This text reveals that there are false gods from whom you cannot receive eternal life for they perish.

Here we see that God is revealing a distinction between Himself and false gods. He is the God of creation. We will see the importance of this as we progress. Further, in Deuteronomy 4:39, it reads: *"Know therefore this day, and consider it in thine heart, that the LORD he is God in heaven above, and upon the earth beneath: there is none else."*

The false gods are nonexistent gods. They have no life in and of themselves and are not our creators. Lucifer is often worshipped either directly or indirectly through God's created things in nature. Satan has been worshipped in the images of the sun, moon, and stars throughout history. These are seen in the Scriptures associated with the high places of Ashtoreth and Baal worship. We will look more at this further on.

Man has a need within him to serve God. It was created in him by his Creator. Yet Satan tries to fill this need by creating gods of his own and thus having man serve him or created things. These are the false gods and they have no life in them. But God is a living God. Jeremiah 10:10 reads: *"But the LORD is the true God, he is the living God, and an everlasting king:"* He is a living God having life within Himself. He was not created or given life. He is the LIVING God. This is why we must know the only true God. For only in the true God will we find life. But how can finite man by searching find God? Is it truly possible?

Perhaps some of the confusion is in understanding what it means to know God. Does it mean to understand all of His purposes for the entire universe? No evidence has been given that God intends to reveal all of His purposes to us. In fact, God's purposes would be too vast and infinite for finite man to comprehend. Does knowing God mean that we will understand God's power or abilities? John reveals in Revelation 19 that: *"the Lord God omnipotent reigneth."* To be omnipotent is defined as being all powerful or having unlimited power. How can finite man understand the unlimited or infinite power of God? Indeed, we cannot. Knowing God is something very different.

Let me give you an example. I know my father. I would be able to recognize him anywhere. I could tell the difference between him and an impostor immediately. I know his voice and the other characteristics he has that make him who he is. Yet, I do not understand all of my father's purposes or abilities even though they are finite. Thus, it can be with our heavenly Father if He intends to reveal Himself to us. We may not fully understand everything there is to know of His purposes and infinite power, but we can know what He is like and be able to recognize Him if He reveals Himself to us. The closer our relationship with Him, the more easily we will recognize Him.

What has inspiration told us? Amos 3:7 states: *"Surely the Lord GOD will do nothing, but he revealeth his secret unto his servants the prophets."* If God's intentions are to reveal Himself to us, He will have first given this truth to His servants, the prophets. Can a man by searching find God? What do the prophets say?

Deuteronomy 4:29 gives us the answer. *"But if from thence thou shalt seek the LORD thy God, thou shalt find him, if thou seek him with all thy heart and with all thy soul."* This theme is repeated throughout the Scriptures. Again, we see this in Jeremiah 29:13. *"And ye shall seek me, and find me, when ye shall search for me with all your heart."* In Matthew 7:7 Christ continued this theme. *"Ask, and it shall be given you; seek, and ye shall find; knock, and it shall be opened unto you."* This is summed up by Paul in

Acts 17:24-28: *"God that made the world and all things therein, seeing that he is Lord of heaven and earth, dwelleth not in temples made with hands; Neither is worshipped with men's hands, as though he needed any thing, seeing he giveth to all life, and breath, and all things;... That they should seek the Lord, if haply they might feel after him, and find him, though he be not far from every one of us: For in him we live, and move, and have our being;"*

The living God, who is the Creator of all things and in whom we have life and breath, can be found if we search for Him with all our hearts. Indeed, He reveals that He is never far from us. God has disclosed to us, through His prophets, His intention to reveal Himself to those who seriously search for Him. He has shown us that He wants to be close to us who are His creation.

Though we cannot understand His omnipotent power and fathomless purposes, we have been given the privilege to know Him and set Him apart from the many false gods created in the minds of men by Satan.

Among the most deadly of the false gods are Satan's counterfeits that closely resemble the true God. They are representations of God that present Him as something other than who and what He is. These are the most dangerous kinds of false gods. They are found among most of the Christian religions today. They present a god that has the same name as

God, the same place of worship as God, and many of the same attributes as God, but they are false gods because they do not have all the attributes of the one true and living God.

These are Satan's masterpieces. They mislead people into thinking that they are serving God when in fact they are deceived. They worship a concept or vision of God that is totally foreign to the Divine Creator. These views of God differ from Him in one or many ways. Even worse, by worshipping Satan's erroneous counterfeits, these deceived people are actually inadvertently worshipping the deceiver himself. Never forget that Satan's goal is to deny God's Son and to be like the Father (the Ancient of Days). Isaiah 14:12-14 states: *"how art thou fallen from heaven, O Lucifer, son of the morning! how art thou cut down to the ground, which didst weaken the nations! For thou hast said in thine heart, I will ascend into heaven, I will exalt my throne above the stars of God: I will sit also upon the mount of the congregation, in the sides of the north: I will ascend above the heights of the clouds; I will be like the most High."*

Satan wants to be worshipped like God. That is why He sets Himself up as false gods that resembles or counterfeits the true and living God. Only will those who know the true God, as revealed in His word, be able to detect the false ones. That is why we are admonished to seek Him with all our heart.

Only the serious searchers will be able to keep the first commandment and have no other gods before Him. They will be the only ones who can tell the false gods from Jehovah, the only true and living God. Are we to seek to know God and understand who He is? The answer is an absolute yes. Only as we seek to understand what God has revealed about Himself will we be able to discern Him from the multitude of false gods or false representations of Him that are planted for our deception.

Not only is this searching to know and understand God our privilege, but it is absolutely essential for our salvation. Some may say at this point that this seems harsh or unreasonable. They feel that God is not particular about such things. Many believe that as long as we worship God in name, go to church, do charity work and do other good things in God's name that it is good enough. In fact, in today's tide of ecumenical soundings of peace and unity, most people say that as long as you worship "God" who cares what religion you are in? Some pursue the idea that all the gods of the different religions are really just the same real God known by different names.

Do the different views of God in each religion really matter to the true God? This type of worship is basically "name or idea" worship. These people call Him by a name and feel that this will be enough and that God isn't concerned about the specifics. But serving God by name or concept alone is not enough. In Matthew 11:23, we are given this warning: *"Many will say to me in that day, Lord, Lord, have we not prophesied in thy name? and in thy name have cast out devils? and in thy name done many wonderful works? And then will I profess unto them, I never knew you: depart from me, ye that work iniquity."* Worshipping an idea of God holds nothing but deception and death for those who do not <u>know</u> God.

We are warned that there will be false gods so we must know the God whose name we confess. Would it honor your earthly father if you called him by any name or if you called anyone you came in contact with his name? Of course, it would not. Neither does it honor your heavenly Father. Yes, you should know and honor His name but that, in and of itself, will not bring eternal life.

We must not allow ourselves to be deceived into believing that God is to be a mystery to us. We must come to know our heavenly Father better than our own earthly father. He has given us the privilege to know Him, unfathomable as it may seem. *"And this is life eternal, that they might <u>know thee</u> the only true God, and Jesus Christ, whom thou hast sent."* The words of Christ in John 17:3 truly echo to our time for they hold the key to eternal life.

Our Heavenly Father is seen in both the Old Testament and New Testament. It is often difficult to distinguish between the Father and Son in the Old Testament because we are told that all things were done though the Son. But with some effort and using the New Testament to clarify some points to some degree it can be done. Many of the works of God in the Old Testament were a combined effort of the Father and the Son. But let's look at the Father remembering that the Son reflects the Father.

His presence has been penned from the beginning to the present. The first four words of the Bible are *"In the beginning God"*. Let's look at the characteristics of this ever present God and what He has revealed about Himself to us in His holy word.

The first attribute we will look at is God's power. In Revelation 19 John the Revelator states that: *"the Lord God omnipotent reigneth."* Remember that to be omnipotent is defined as being all powerful or having unlimited power. This includes the power to create and to give life. This is the first attribute revealed in the Scriptures. In Genesis 1:1, we read that *"In the beginning God created the heaven and the earth."* This fact is supported throughout the Scriptures. In Isaiah 42:5, we are told: *"Thus saith God the LORD, he that created the heavens, and stretched them out; he that spread forth the earth, and that which cometh out of it; he that giveth breath unto the people upon it, and spirit to them that walk therein: I the LORD have called thee in righteousness, and will hold thine hand, and will keep thee..."*

Through His power, God also created man. This is clearly seen in the text above and in Genesis where we are told that God created man from the dust of the ground. At this point some may feel that this is in error for the Scriptures also reveal that all things were created by Jesus. In Ephesians 3:9 we read: *"And to make all men see what is the fellowship of the mystery, which from the beginning of the world hath been hid in God, who created all things by Jesus Christ:"* We will look closely at this in the upcoming chapters. For now suffice it to say that God the Father is truly all powerful. Jeremiah 32:17 reads: *"Ah Lord GOD! behold, thou hast made the heaven and the earth by thy great power and stretched out arm, and there is nothing too hard for thee:"*

Another attribute that is revealed is that God has total knowledge and wisdom. 1Samuel 2:3 says that: *"the LORD is a God of knowledge."* This is clear throughout the Scriptures. Proverbs 2:6 also reveals this. *"For the LORD giveth wisdom: out of his mouth cometh knowledge and understanding."* This is again seen in Proverbs 3:19-20 which says that: *"The LORD by wisdom hath founded the earth; by understanding hath he established the heavens. By his knowledge the depths are broken up, and the clouds drop down the dew."*

Yet, another attribute is that God is omnipresent. He sees all of us and what we are doing. Proverbs 5:21 says that: *"the ways of man are before the eyes of the LORD, and he pondereth all his goings."* In Proverbs 15:3, we read that: *"The eyes of the LORD are in every place, beholding the evil and the good."* Man cannot hide his ways from God. This omnipresent attribute of God is important and will be looked at in greater detail further on.

I could place pages and pages of text here that declare that God is all powerful, full of wisdom, always present, and the source of all knowledge. But the point has already been made. Most people have no problem understanding and believing that God has these abilities but herein lays a problem. Most, if not all, of the counterfeit gods are also portrayed in the same way. Most of the gods of the world's religions are also believed to be all powerful, all knowing, and possessing all wisdom and knowledge.

God would have to reveal more of Himself to us to help us to recognize and differentiate Him from the others. This is exactly what He has done. God does not want us to be in the dark concerning Himself. Some of His traits are copied, but He never allows all of them to be emulated. Some of what God reveals about Himself differs greatly from the counterfeit gods as we will begin to see.

Chapter 4
God is One

In Deuteronomy 6:4-5, God reveals another of His attributes. Surprisingly, this is the one that there is more confusion on than any of the other attributes we have studied so far. Yet, it should not be. It is very straight forward. We read: *"Hear, O Israel: The LORD our God is <u>one</u> LORD: And thou shalt love the LORD thy God with all thine heart, and with all thy soul, and with all thy might."* Here God reveals that He is <u>one God</u>. This is not a chance wording on His part. Remember that in Deuteronomy 4:39 it reads: *"Know therefore this day, and consider it in thine heart, that the LORD he is God in heaven above, and upon the earth beneath: there is none else."* There is no mention of two, three or more gods. The religions that present polytheistic views of God are not in harmony with the Scriptures. Psalm 89:18 tells us that: *"the LORD is our defense; and the Holy One of Israel is our king."* The Scriptures use the term "Holy ONE of Israel" over 30 times.

In Mark 12:28-30, Christ reaffirms this concept. We read: *"Which is the first commandment of all? And Jesus answered him, The first of all the commandments is, Hear, O Israel; The Lord our God is one Lord: And thou shalt love the Lord thy God with all thy heart, and with all thy soul, and with all thy mind, and with all thy strength: this is the first commandment."* Note that this was emphasized as the first and greatest commandment. It identifies a very important aspect of God which He wants us to know. It is ONE GOD that we are admonished to worship, not three.

Many Christians today mistakenly believe that this refers to a triune picture of three gods in one. They believe that the Father, the Son, and the Holy Spirit all comprise one God. This God union is called the trinity. But there are several problems for this theory presented in the Scriptures. Let me point out here that the author is not denying the reality of the Father, Son, or Holy Spirit so let's clarify the Scriptures teachings. First and foremost is the absence of the term trinity, triune, or any other like term in the Scriptures. It is simply not there.

Another problem is that it is inconsistent with several texts. Let's look at some. The first is John 17:3 which states: *"And this is life eternal, that they might know thee the only true God, and Jesus Christ, whom thou hast sent."*

Note that when Christ identifies the only true living God, He does not include Himself in the "only true God" but identifies Himself separately. In Hebrews 9:24 we read that: *"Christ is not entered into the holy places made with hands, which are the figures of the true; but into heaven itself, now to appear in the presence of God for us:"* Here we again see that Jesus Christ is not included in the term "God", even after His ascension. Note again the absence of any reference to a trinity god. We see this over and over in the New Testament where Jesus does not include Himself in the term God. Yet, we know that He is divine and held as an equal by the Father. We will explore this apparent paradox in further detail shortly.

Where the confusion begins is the fact that there are three references to deity. One is the Father, the second is Christ, and the third is the Holy Spirit (sometimes also referred to as the Holy Ghost or Spirit of God). The surface reader assumes that each comprises part of a triune godhead and thus many are deceived. Assumptions are probably the greatest source error there is.

The reader may be surprised to find that the source of this confusion is very old. The trinitarian doctrine, that is so prevalent in the Protestant denominations today, is in fact nothing more than a carryover of an ancient Roman Catholic doctrine. Unlike Protestant churches, many saints are prayed to in the Catholic Church. The Pope himself assumes to have the authority of God and is thus called the Vicar of Christ. Their priests even presume to be able to forgive sin. The Catholic Church's belief that it has the right to add to or change the Bible was one of the key problems that brought on the reformation. Yet, these doctrines were not original to Catholicism, but can be traced all the way to Egyptian and Babylonian occult practices and beliefs.

Among the beliefs in Protestantism today is a polytheistic view of God. This is a carryover of doctrines that were spawned by the combining of Pagan Rome and Papal Rome in the fourth and fifth centuries AD.

During the centuries that followed Christ's ministry here on earth, the Christian church went through many trials and attacks. First, they were tortured and killed by pagan Rome. Many were torn apart by wild animals before demon filled throngs in the Roman Coliseum. The church was forced into the catacombs, hiding in caves and tombs below Rome. The atrocities were unthinkable; yet God's truth survived and even prospered during those times of persecution. When Satan saw that he could not defeat it with force, he changed his methods. If he could not defeat them openly, then he would infiltrate them with error.

Suddenly, the Christian faith became the official religion of Rome. To appease the pagan population of Rome, many of the pagan beliefs were incorporated into the Christian religion. Suddenly the Roman gods where brought into the church under the guise as disciples and apostles. The same masses that once bowed to the pagan gods now bowed to the same images with new names.

This practice continued as other truths became violated and corrupted. The Sabbath commandment of God, that had been in place since He finished His creation of earth and hallowed the seventh day (Saturday), was replaced with the pagan day of sun worship (Sunday, the venerable day of the Sun). Righteousness by faith in Jesus alone was replaced with righteousness by works. Thus, the rise of Papal Rome and the mix of pagan and Christian beliefs were established that we now see in the Papal church. The triune belief in God was nothing more than a carryover of the pagan belief in a triune god represented by the trident carried by Neptune, one of the Roman gods. From there, it could be traced all the way back to Egypt with the worship of Isis, Osiris, and Horus. It was one of the founding doctrines of this new Christian/pagan hybrid religion called Catholicism.

If there is any doubt on this matter, that this is indeed a Roman Catholic doctrine, read the following statement. It is taken from the book entitled "The Handbook for Today's Catholic" written by the Roman Catholic Church. It reads on page 11, **"The mystery of the Trinity is the central doctrine of Catholic faith. Upon it are based all the other teachings of the Church. "**

This is not meant to be an attack of the Catholic people. Many of the most sincere Christians I know are Catholic. It is only to provide a historical background to the errors that have crept into the church through Satan's efforts to infiltrate it. Sadly enough, he has been very successful in this mission. This single error (the trinity Doctrine), introduced into the church almost 1700 years ago, has misled and confused more people than any other false doctrine employed by Satan. As time has progressed, various views of the trinity have been spawned by different churches and communities of faith.

In Catholicism, the trinity doctrine sees Christ as an eternal generation or procession from the Father. Quoting from the website Catholic Planet we read: *"The Father-Son-Spirit is one God. The First Person of the Trinity does not proceed from the Second Person or the Third Person. The First Person of the Trinity is First and so cannot proceed from anyone. The Second Person of the Trinity proceeds solely from the First Person of the Trinity. The Second Person is not primary, but secondary. The Father's knowledge of Himself is the Son. 232 All that the Son is comes from the Father. The Son depends entirely upon the Father. Therefore, the Father is greater than the Son: "….for the Father is greater than I." (Jn 14:28). Christ could not have been referring merely to His human nature, when He said that the Father is greater than the Son. [As Aquinas claimed in the Summa Theologica, First Part, Question 42, Article 4, Reply to Objection 1.] The Human and Divine Natures of Christ are united in One Person, so Christ would not have spoken of His Human Nature as if it were separate, He would not have compared His Human Nature alone, which in itself is finite, to the infinite First Person of the Trinity. The Son said that the Father is greater than the Son, not because the Son took on a Human Nature, but because the First Person of the Trinity is truly greater than the Second Person of the Trinity. The Father is greater than the Son, because the Son obtains everything He has from the Father."*

Here we see a doctrine where Christ is always being generated by the Father and has no life in and of Himself. He is also seen as not equal with the Father. This is not in harmony with the Scriptures. In Hebrews, chapter one, He is clearly pointed out to be equal with the Father.

In many Protestant religions, a different view of the trinity is presented. They see the Father, the Son, and the Holy Spirit as co-eternal and co-equal. In the book <u>Seventh-day Adventists Believe</u>, it reads as follows: **"There is one God: Father, Son, and Holy Spirit, a unity of three co-eternal Persons. God is immortal, all-powerful, all-knowing, above all, and ever present. He is infinite and beyond human comprehension, yet known through His self-revelation. He is forever worthy of worship, adoration, and service by the whole creation."** Here, we have swung from one extreme to the other. The above statement of beliefs shows that Christ received nothing from His Father. Again, this is not in harmony with Hebrews chapter one where Christ clearly receives an inheritance from the Father. The problem still exists that the <u>word "trinity" or doctrine of the trinity</u> is simply not supported in the Scriptures.

At this point many will state that what we are presenting is an old Arian doctrine, so let's look closer at this. The man Arius was born sometime around AD 250 and died in AD 336. He was a Christian Presbyter from Alexandria, Egypt. It has been handed down as fact by the Catholic Church that he taught a doctrine claiming that Christ was a created being and thus only a created Son of God. This supposed teaching denied that Christ was God by substance and was nothing more than a promoted creation. What Arius actually taught is unknown because Emperor Constantine had all his writings condemned to the flames and none of Arius' authentic teachings or writings survived.

Arius was viewed by the Catholic Church as being too liberal in his theology and viewed as a heretic. There are, however, other historians who disagree and some feel that he was actually quite conservative. History shows that much of his trouble was caused by his open opposition to the way that the church was mixing Greek paganism into its own theology. This mixing of paganism into the church is undeniable and is clearly visible still today. It is believed by many that Arius actually did not deny the

Divinity of Christ but actually saw him as the true Son of God, born of the very substance of God and thus thought it not robbery to be equal with God. Further, it is conjectured that he believed that in the ages past before the beginning of any created thing that He was born of the very substance of the Father. Whatever the truth was, Rome fully opposed it and his true teachings died with him.

It was over this debate that the first council Nicaea was convened by the Roman Emperor Constantine in AD 325. Its mission was to settle this debate and set forth a statement verifying the church's position on the relationship of Jesus to the Father. The final outcome was summed up in the following.

1. Jesus Christ is described as "God from God, Light from Light, true God from true God," proclaiming his divinity. When all light sources were natural, the essence of light was considered to be identical, regardless of its form.
2. Jesus Christ is said to be "begotten, not made", asserting his co-eternalness with God, and confirming it by stating his role in the Creation. Basically, they were saying that Jesus was God, and God's Son, not a creation of God, but a generation of God.
3. He is said to be "from the substance of the Father," in direct opposition to Arianism. Eusebius of Caesarea ascribes the term homoousios, or

consubstantial, i.e., "of the same substance" (of the Father), to Constantine who, on this particular point, may have chosen to exercise his authority.

This statement confirmed the deity of Christ but still left confusion on the relationship between the Father and the Son and the issue of Christ's eternal birth. The Bible teaches that God is one God and that He has a Son, Jesus Christ. There is no mention of a trinity. Who or what the Holy Spirit is we have not yet addressed, but we will further on. For many this may seem ridiculous or even blasphemous, but I ask that you prayerfully continue with this study. An understanding of the relationship between the Father and the Son and the truth about the Holy Spirit (as established by the SDA church founders) is essential for our salvation. We, as the remnant people, should not remain rooted in error when the truth is more fabulous and holds the key to a rudimentary understanding of God. So let's take a closer look at the Son of God.

"*In the beginning was the Word, and the Word was with God, and the Word was God. The same was in the beginning with God. All things were made by him; and without him was not anything made that was made. In him was life; and the life was the light of men.*" (John 1:1-2) Christ was the Living Word. He was the Son of God. The New Testament reveals this time and time again. But what was His relationship with the Father? Was He a co-equal or co-eternal

God with the Father? Many take the above text to imply this, but is that what it teaches? Let's examine this carefully.

It starts with the words "In the beginning" but the beginning of what? The text gives the answer. It is the beginning of creation. We saw earlier that God the Father created all things by His Son Jesus. (Ephesians 3:7-9) This text reemphasizes this. Thus, when we see Genesis 1:1 state that in the beginning God created the heavens and the earth we understand that this was the work of God through His Son.

Proverbs 8 sheds more light on this. In this Proverb, we see the Father and Son presented in the Old Testament. The Son is referred to here as Wisdom. We will begin with verse 14 and look at this very important text point by point along with supporting texts. This will take a few minutes but let's explore it carefully.

"Counsel is mine, and sound wisdom: I am understanding; I have strength. By me kings reign, and princes decree justice." The Scriptures refer to Christ as King of kings and Lord of lords. This is seen in 1 Timothy 6:15-16 *"Which in his times he shall shew, who is the blessed and only Potentate, the King of kings, and Lord of lords; Who only hath immortality, dwelling in the light which no man can approach unto; whom no man hath seen, nor can see: to whom be honour and power* everlasting. Amen." It is also shown in Revelation 17:14 and Revelation 19:16 *"These shall make war with the Lamb, and the Lamb shall overcome them: for he is Lord of lords, and King of kings ... And I heard as it were the voice of mighty thunderings, saying, Alleluia: for the Lord God omnipotent reigneth."*

"By me princes rule, and nobles, even all the judges of the earth. I love them that love me; and those that seek me early shall find me." Remember that we are admonished to seek the Lord with all our heart. We studied this theme earlier. In John 19:11, Jesus points this out to Pilot when He stated: *"Thou couldest have no power at all against me, except it were given thee from above".* All kings and rulers of this world are only in power because Jesus allows them to be. Daniel told us in Daniel 2:21-22: *" Daniel answered and said, Blessed be the name of God for ever and ever: for wisdom and might are his: And he changeth the times and the seasons: he removeth kings, and setteth up kings: he giveth wisdom unto the wise, and knowledge to them that know understanding."*

Continuing on in Proverbs 8 we read: **"Riches and honour are with me; yea, durable riches and righteousness."** There are too many Scriptures to put here concerning this but in Ephesians 1:7,18 we read: "In whom we have redemption through his blood, the forgiveness of sins, according to the riches of his grace ... that ye may know what is the hope of his *calling, and what the riches of the glory of his inheritance in the saints"* Other texts include Ephesians 3:18, Romans 9:23, Philippians 4:19, and Colossians 1:27 just to name a few. Jesus is the source of riches in righteousness. In Revelation, He says "buy of me gold, tried in the fire."

Moving on in Proverbs 8:19, **"My fruit is better than gold, yea, than fine gold; and my revenue than choice silver. I lead in the way of righteousness, in the midst of the paths of judgment:"** Again, there are many texts that point this to Christ, but see 2 Peter 2:9, Hebrews 9:27-28, and 2 Corinthians 5:10. The Bible teaches us that it is Christ's righteousness that protects and surrounds us in the judgment. Our righteousness will avail us nothing. *"But we are all as an unclean thing, and all our righteousnesses are as filthy rags; and we all do fade as a leaf; and our iniquities, like the wind, have taken us away."* (Isaiah 64:6)

"That I may cause those that love me to inherit substance; and I will fill their treasures." (Proverbs 8:20) It should be plain by now that the Scriptures are speaking of Jesus. Now read the next verse carefully. **"The LORD possessed me in the beginning of his way, before his works of old. I was set up from everlasting, from the beginning, or ever the earth was. When there were no depths, <u>I was brought forth</u>; when there were no fountains abounding with water. Before the mountains were**

settled, before the hills <u>was I brought forth</u>: While as yet he had not made the earth, nor the fields, nor the highest part of the dust of the world." This is a text that Satan did not want you to see. It cuts right into the heart of his trinity doctrine. It clearly declares that Jesus was brought forth as the Son to God. One must not get confused here and believe that Christ was created. The Bible does not teach that He was created. Christ is not a created being. He is the actual Son of God.

Let's read on. *"When he prepared the heavens, I was there: when he set a compass upon the face of the depth: When he established the clouds above: when he strengthened the fountains of the deep: When he gave to the sea his decree, that the waters should not pass his commandment: when he appointed the foundations of the earth: Then I was by him, as <u>one brought up</u> with him: and I was daily his delight, rejoicing always before him; Rejoicing in the habitable part of his earth; and my delights were with the sons of men."*

Here Christ paints a remarkable picture of His relationship with His Father. First, He reveals that before anything was created, sometime in eternity past, He was brought forth from the Father. He, then, describes Himself being brought up by Him in a beautiful father/son relationship. This drives a nail into the coffin of the trinity doctrine. The trinity doctrine expresses the belief that Jesus is either an eternal generation of the Father or is a co-eternal brother with God. Yet, the Scriptures say otherwise.

Lest there be confusion on the relationship of the Father and Son, E J Waggoner in his book <u>Christ and His Righteousness</u> wrote: **'The Scriptures declare that Christ is "the only begotten son of God." He is begotten, not created. As to when He was begotten, it is not for us to inquire, nor could our minds grasp it if we were told. The prophet Micah tells us all that we can know about it in these words, "But thou, Bethlehem Ephratah, though thou be little among the thousands of Judah, yet out of thee shall He come forth unto Me that is to be ruler in Israel; whose goings forth have been from of old, from the days of eternity." Micah 5:2, margin. There was a time when Christ proceeded forth and came from God, from the bosom of the Father (John 8:42; 1:18), but that time was so far back in the days of eternity that to finite comprehension it is practically without beginning."** <u>CR</u> Chapter 5

As was shown earlier, Ellen White wrote: "**Christ, the Word, the only begotten of God, was one with the eternal Father--one in nature, in character, in purpose-- <u>the only being</u> that could enter into all the counsels and purposes of God. "His name shall be called Wonderful, Counselor, The mighty God, The everlasting Father, The Prince of Peace." Isaiah 9:6. His "goings forth have been from of old, from everlasting." Micah 5:2. And the Son of God declares concerning Himself: "<u>The Lord possessed Me in the beginning of His way,</u>**

before His works of old. I was set up from everlasting. . . . When He appointed the foundations of the earth: then I was by Him, as one brought up with Him: and I was daily His delight, rejoicing always before Him." Proverbs 8:22-30." PP 34 Here she clearly shows that Proverbs 8 is speaking of the pre-incarnate Christ being the Son of God.

We will look at this unique relationship in other texts, but let's finish Proverbs 8. *"Now therefore hearken unto me, O ye children: for blessed are they that keep my ways. Hear instruction, and be wise, and refuse it not. Blessed is the man that heareth me, watching daily at my gates, waiting at the posts of my doors. For whoso findeth me findeth life, and shall obtain favour of the LORD."* In John 14:6, Jesus speaking of Himself states *"...I am the way, the truth, and the life..."* There can be no mistaking that this text is pointing to Christ and Him alone. This is not the only text that points to this truth.

In Hebrews 1:1-6, we read: **"God, who at sundry times and in divers manners spake in time past unto the fathers by the prophets, Hath in these last days spoken unto us by his Son, whom he hath appointed heir of all things, by whom also he made the worlds; Who being the brightness of his glory, and the express image of his person, and upholding all things by the word of his power, when he had by himself purged our sins, sat down on the right hand** *of the Majesty on high; Being made so much better than the angels, as he hath <u>by inheritance</u> obtained a more excellent name than they. For unto which of the angels said he at any time, Thou art my Son, <u>this day have I begotten Thee</u>? And again, I will be to him a Father, and he shall be to me a Son? <u>And again, when he bringeth in the first begotten into the world</u>, he saith, And let all the angels of God worship him."*

This is a clear statement about God the Father and His relationship to His Son. Note that He refers to Him as the first begotten, before He came into the world. This supports what we read in Proverbs 8. John 3:16, which we all know well, reveals that God loved the world and gave His only begotten Son. When He gave Him He was already called His only begotten. Ellen White in Patriarchs and Prophets testifies to this when she wrote: **"The plan of salvation had been laid before the creation of the earth; for Christ is "the Lamb slain from the foundation of the world" (Revelation 13:8); yet it was a struggle, even with the King of the universe, to yield up <u>His Son</u> to die for the guilty race. But "God so loved the world, that He gave His only-begotten Son, that whosoever believeth in Him should not perish, but have everlasting life."** (John 3:16)

Paul, in Hebrews 1, further differentiates Jesus from the angels by reason of His inheritance. If Christ was co-eternal with the Father, why need an inheritance? The very word describes something a son receives of his father. Let's read on: *"And of the angels he saith, Who maketh his angels spirits, and his ministers a flame of fire. But unto the Son he saith, Thy throne, O God, is for ever and ever: a sceptre of righteousness is the sceptre of thy kingdom."* Jesus is God by substance from His very birth.

The book of Revelation calls Christ the Alpha and the Omega, the beginning and the end. The Bible simply teaches that Jesus is the true Son of God. He was born of His Father in ages past and by Him God created all things. What He received, He received as an inheritance from His Father.

Does this make Him anything less than divine and worthy of our worship? Of course it does not. What we see is why the Father is referred to as the one God. We see why Jesus refers to Him as the only true God. God is God by substance alone. He is the Ancient of Days, without beginning or end. He received nothing from another source. He was the originator and complete within Himself. Jesus, however, is God by the name and substance He inherited by birth. He inherited the brightness of His Father's glory and the express image of His Father. Yes, both are God but not co-eternal, and not co-equal. For the Father is God by substance alone and the Son by the inherited substance from His Father.

Christ's mission was and still is to reveal His Father and to bring glory and honor to Him in all of His creation. At this point again the distinction must be made. The Scriptures do not say He was created like us. We were created in the image of God, but we were not born of God. Neither were the angels. Only Jesus was born of His Father and, by the very nature of what He was, received His inheritance. Thus we see in John 3:35: *"The Father loveth the Son, and hath given all things into his hand."*

Finally, we see that they are one in purpose and that God has set His Son upon a throne to be worshipped. Their thrones are side by side for Christ: *"sat down on the right hand of the Majesty on high."* We are told that He (Christ) shall reign forever and ever. This truth in no way attacks the divinity of Christ and reveals the deep truth about God and His Son. This relationship must be understood if the error of the last great omega of apostasy is to be avoided and the true nature of righteousness by faith is to be revealed. For in the understanding of their relationship we will find the truth concerning the Holy Spirit.

Chapter 5
Source of Confusion

Although there is much confusion on this subject in the church today, there was no confusion on this point by the founding fathers of the SDA Church. What our pioneers believed about God's Son can be seen by various statements given by our founding fathers.

JAMES WHITE "*The Father is the greatest in that he is first. The Son is next in authority because He has been given all things.*" Review and Herald, Jan. 4, 1881.

J.N. ANDREWS "*And as to the Son of God, he would be excluded also, for he had God for his Father, and did, at some point in the eternity of the past, have beginning of days. So that if we use Paul's language in an absolute sense, it would be impossible to find but one being in the universe, and that is God the Father, who is without father, or mother, or descent, or beginning of days, or end of life.*" Review and Herald, Sept. 7, 1869.

C.W. STONE "*The Word, then, is Christ. This text speaks of his origin. He is the only begotten of the Father. Just how he came into existence, the Bible does not inform us any more definitely; but by this expression and several of a similar kind in the*

Scriptures, we may believe that Christ came into existence in a manner different from that in which other beings first appeared; that he sprang from the Father's being in a way not necessary for us to understand"* The Captain Of Our Salvation, 1886, p. 17.

E.J. WAGGONER *"In arguing the perfect equality of the Father and the Son, and the fact that Christ is in very nature God, we do not design to be understood as teaching that the Father was not before the Son. It should not be necessary to guard this point, lest some should think that the Son existed as soon as the Father; yet some go to that extreme, which adds nothing to the dignity of Christ, but rather detracts from the honor due him, since many throw the whole thing away rather than accept a theory so obviously out of harmony with the language of Scripture, that Jesus is the only begotten Son of God. He was begotten, not created. He is of the substance of the Father, so that in his very nature he is God; and since this is so 'It pleased the Father that in him should all fullness dwell.' Col. 1:19...While both are of the same nature, the Father is first in point of time. He is also greater in that he had no beginning, while Christ's personality had a beginning."* Signs of the Times, April 8, 1889, p. 214.

W.W. PRESCOTT *"As Christ was twice born, once in eternity, the only begotten of the Father, and again here in the flesh, thus uniting the divine* *with the human in that second birth, so we, who have been born once already in the flesh, are to have the second birth, being born again of the Spirit, in order that our experience may be the same, the human and the divine being joined in a life union."* Review and Herald, April 14, 1896, p. 232.

A.T. *JONES* **"He was born of the Holy Ghost. In other words, Jesus Christ was born again. He came from heaven, God's firstborn, to the earth, and was born again, But all in Christ's work goes by opposites for us: he, the sinless one, was made to be sin, in order that we might be made the righteousness of God in him. He, the living one, the prince and author of life, died that we might live. He whose goings forth have been from the days of eternity, the first-born of God, was born again, in order that we might be born again. If Jesus Christ had never been born again, could you and I have ever been born again? No. But he was born again, from the world of righteousness into the world of sin; that we might be born again, from the world of sin into the world of righteousness. He was born again, and was made partaker of the human nature, that we might be born again, and so made partakers of the divine nature. He was born again, unto earth, unto sin, and unto man, that we might be born again unto heaven, unto righteousness, and unto God."** Review and Herald, Aug. 1, 1899, (Lessons on Faith p. 154.)

J.M. STEPHENSON *"To be the only begotten Son of God must be understood in a different sense than to be a Son by creation; for in that sense all the creatures he has made are sons. Nor can it refer to his miraculous conception, with the virgin Mary, by the Holy Ghost; because he is represented by this endearing title more than four thousand years before his advent in the village of Bethlehem. Moreover, he is represented as being exalted far above the highest orders of men and angels in his primeval nature. He must therefore be understood as being the Son of God in a much higher sense than any other being. His being the only begotten of the Father supposes that none except him were thus begotten; hence he is, in truth and verity the only begotten Son of God; and as such he must be Divine; that is, be a partaker of the Divine nature. This term expresses his highest, and most exalted nature...*

"The idea of Father and Son supposes priority of the existence of the one, and the subsequent existence of the other. To say that the Son is as old as his Father, is a palpable contradiction of terms. It is a natural impossibility for the Father to be as young as the Son, or the Son to be as old as the Father. If it be said that this term is only used in an accommodated sense, it still remains to be accounted for, why the Father should use as the uniform title of the highest, and most endearing relation between himself and our Lord, a term which, in its uniform signification, would contradict

the very idea he wished to convey. If the inspired writers had wished to convey the idea of the coetaneous existence, and eternity of the Father and Son, they could not possibly have used more incompatible terms. And of this, Trinitarians, had the honesty to acknowledge, in the conclusion of his work on the Son-ship of Christ, that, 'in the order of nature, the Father must have existed Before the Son.'" Review and Herald, Nov. 14, 1854.

D.M. CANRIGHT *"'For God so loved the world that he gave his only begotten Son. According to this, Jesus Christ is begotten of God in a sense that no other being is; else he could not be his only begotten Son. Angels are called sons of God, and so are righteous men; but Christ is his Son in a higher sense, in a closer relation, than either of these. God made men and angels out of materials already created. He is the author of their existence, their Creator, hence their Father. But Jesus Christ was begotten of the Father's own substance. He was not created out of material as the angels and other creatures were. He is truly and emphatically the 'Son of God,'...Heb.1:1-8 quoted."* Review and Herald, June 18, 1867

Many more could be quoted but the point is clear. Our forefathers held a different view than what our church's Seventh-day Adventist Believe book now teaches on the nature of Christ. This may be a shock to many an SDA believer, but it is true. Many of our church leaders know this very well. On the website maranathamedia.com, Blair Andrew writes the following article addressing this. I have included it here in full. It is lengthy but it lays out the issues facing the remnant church on this point very well. Other than simple spelling and punctuation corrections, it is quoted directly from his website.

"As Seventh-day Adventists, we have long regarded ourselves as the "people of the Book." However, when doctrinal differences arise, what do we do? Often, when agreement cannot be found using Scripture alone, quotations from the Spirit of Prophecy are resorted to in an attempt to resolve the issue. Both sides of the argument usually end up at a loss to know why their point of view is not as clear to the other party as it is to them! We forget Ellen White's words when she said: "The spirit in which you come to the investigation of the Scriptures *will determine the character of the assistant at your side.* Angels from the world of light will be with those who in humility of heart seek for divine guidance. . . . But if the heart is filled with prejudice, Satan is beside you, *and he will set the plain statements of God's word in a perverted light."* – TM, *p.108*. (Emphasis supplied)

How careful we need to be then, in light of the ongoing controversy surrounding the Trinity! The spirit in which we investigate the doctrinal change from non-Trinitarianism to Trinitarianism is one issue we need to consider carefully and prayerfully. There have been many controversies in Adventism during its brief history. Perhaps the current debate over the Trinity is the most far reaching of them all. Obviously, *who* we worship, is more important than *when* and *how* we worship. This whole issue of worship will continue to shake our church, whether we like it or not; and we know it will eventually shake the whole world.

Whenever something like this arises which involves church history, I am reminded of another Ellen White statement we all know so well, "We have nothing to fear for the future, except as we shall forget the way the Lord has led us, *and His teaching in our past history.*" LS, p.196. (Emphasis supplied)

This statement affirming the teachings established by our church pioneers is quite clear. God led the Great Second Advent Movement and He has remained consistent in all His teaching in our past history. It is miraculous that God has preserved the truth through thousands of years, without contradiction. Truth has shone down through the ages, from Eden to Abraham, on to the Israelites, clarified further by Christ Himself, and right through to the Advent Movement. Now we find ourselves in a church which advocates teachings which appear to contradict the past history. Is it new light, commonly termed progressive revelation, as many claim? Or is it error as others suggest?

When and how? It is a well-documented fact that the early Seventh-day Adventist Pioneers were categorically non-Trinitarian and the modern Seventh-day Adventist church today is clearly a Trinitarian church. The current understanding of our church's history is basically as follows:

The Adventist Pioneers were wrong in their non-Trinitarian beliefs and teachings. As God has revealed more light to us as a people, (what might be termed progressive revelation) modern Adventism has grown and advanced, walking in the light, desiring to spiritually move forward in harmony with God's truth. We now have more truth than ever before, and are faithfully preparing the world for the coming of Christ, and His people for translation.

This sounds good, but a question that has not been well addressed nor adequately answered is this: "*When* and *how* did this major doctrinal change come about?"

The vast majority of Seventh-day Adventist scholars and theologians attribute the doctrinal change from non-Trinitarianism to Trinitarianism to the writings of Ellen G. White (i.e. specifically in a book prepared for the non-Adventist market, "The

Desire of Ages"). William Johnson in the *Review* put the explanation for change in these words:

"Adventist beliefs have changed over the years under the impact of 'present truth.' Most startling is the teaching regarding Jesus Christ, our Savior and Lord. Many of the pioneers, including James White, J.N. Andrews, Uriah Smith, and J. H. Waggoner, held to an Arian or semi-Arian view - that is, the Son at some point in time before the Creation of our world was generated by the Father. Only gradually did this false doctrine give way to the biblical truth, and largely under the impact of Ellen White's writings in statements such as: 'In Christ is life, original, unborrowed, underived' (The Desire of Ages, p. 530)." - W.G. Johnson, Adventist Review, Jan. 6, 1994 pg. 10.

Gilbert Valentine stated it this way: "When did the change to Trinitarianism occur? As Jerry Moon points out, 'an irreversible paradigm shift' occurred in the Adventist Church in the 1890's, spurred along by the church's publication of Ellen White's *The Desire of Ages* in 1898. This influential book on the life of Christ reflected Mrs. White's own developing understanding and called attention 'to Scriptures whose significance had been overlooked.' Its publication contributed to a 'complete reversal' of Adventist thinking on the Trinity, and it became a kind of 'continental divide.'" – Gilbert M. Valentine,

Ministry Magazine, May 2005, p.14, Art. How Clear Views of Jesus Developed.

Erwin Gane in his summary on Anti-Trinitarianism, stated: "What changed the prevailing Seventh-day Adventist view from Arianism to Trinitarianism? The evidence would indicate that it was the publication of the Trinitarian declarations of Ellen G. White in the last decades of the nineteenth century that initiated the change. It would appear that she wrote little before the early 1890s which could have led to serious questioning of the prevailing Arian view. Most of her statements which appeared before 1890 could have been interpreted to agree with the Arian doctrine. But from the early 1890s on, Ellen G. White produced increasingly unequivocal Trinitarian statements. She did not contradict any position she had formerly taken." – Erwin Gane, Anti-Trinitarianism, chapter XVI, Summary.

George Knight in *Ministry* gave this explanation: "It was Ellen White whose writings led the way in the theological shift. Unlike her experience in the post-1844 period, during which she followed the lead of her husband and Bates in the formulation of the distinctive Adventist doctrines, in the 1890's she was at the forefront of the action, related to theological reformulation, through her major writings on Christ and His teachings. . . . it should be obvious to our readers that Adventism has experienced major theological change across the course of its history and that Ellen White had a role in that change." – G. Knight, Ministry, Oct, 1993. p.10,11. Art. Adventists and Change.

This is the prevailing belief of most Adventists today. However, if the above argument is true, it needs careful consideration. Questions arise which need answers. Questions such as:

1. Why is there no record of a vision or dream from the Lord telling Ellen White to change her views and to correct the views of the denomination to accept the Trinity doctrine?

2. As the prophetess to the last-days remnant church, wouldn't she have been duty bound to go to the leaders of our denomination at the time, and explain to them their error? Why did she not call a meeting of the leaders and scholars of the church at the time and do this? There is no record of such a meeting.

3. Why did she not write private "testimonies" to any of the leaders of the Church, clarifying the necessity to change to Trinitarianism? To allow people to continue to believe and teach error, and then just publish a book, and leave it to gradually change the mind of whoever might read it, without even saying to anybody "we were wrong on this matter"; was that Ellen White's way?

4. Why did she choose to publish her new views in an evangelistic book designed for the general public, as if she wanted the world to think we were Trinitarian? Would not this be deceptive on her part, and against Gospel Order (Matt 18:15-17)? The method she chose to employ on this issue opened the whole church to public embarrassment, scandal and controversy. But nothing came of it at the time. Why is this so?

5. It is a known fact that The Desire of Ages was largely compiled from her existing writings, put together by herself and her assistants. It was also a book which took some years to compile. There was no reaction when these so-called "Trinitarian statements" were first published in the years leading up to 1898; why then in more recent years do scholars make such strong statements about the importance of the book in changing the direction of the whole denomination; and yet these statements made very little impact on the minds of leaders, scholars and teachers within the denomination for many years. Why is this so?

6. Why, five years after the publication of The Desire of Ages, in 1903, did Ellen White pen these words:

"Many will depart from the faith and give heed to seducing spirits. Patriarchs and Prophets and The Great Controversy are books that are especially adapted to those who have newly come to the faith, that they may be established in the truth. The dangers are pointed out that should be avoided by the churches. Those who become thoroughly acquainted with the lessons in these books will see the dangers before them and will be able to discern the plain, straight path marked out for them. They will be kept from strange paths. They will make straight paths for their feet, lest the lame be turned out of the way." "In <u>Desire of Ages</u>, <u>Patriarchs and Prophets</u>, <u>The Great Controversy</u>, and in <u>Daniel and the Revelation</u>, there is precious instruction.

"These books must be regarded as of special importance, and every effort should be made to get them before the people." - Ellen G. White, Letter 229, 1903. <u>Evangelism</u>, p. 36

To non-Trinitarians this poses no problem for all are regarded as good, non-Trinitarian, books. But to a Trinitarian, these books are known to contain clear, unequivocal statements which are regarded as non-Trinitarian; even *Arian* in their thinking!

7. Why didn't Ellen White organize (see to it), in the 17 years after <u>Desire of Ages</u> was published, that all of her books be re-edited to remove any non-Trinitarian thoughts, thus aiding the church along on the path of truth?

8. For a prophetess who supposedly borrowed some terms, expressions and sometimes whole sentences from other writers, why was she meticulously careful never even once to borrow the term 'Trinity', or to state it in no uncertain terms?

9. Why did she not rebuke the two messengers of the 1888 Message during the 1890's on their views on the Sonship of Christ, the outpouring of the Holy Spirit in the Latter Rain and Loud Cry, as they clearly differed from the Trinitarian position?

But what about . . . ? Are these valid questions? Do you have answers to them? And then there is this. In <u>Ministry</u> magazine, dated February 1983, the Adventist leadership published a statement of present understanding on *"The inspiration and authority of the Ellen G. White writings."* Under the heading *"Denials"* we read:

3. *"We do not believe that the writings of Ellen White function as the foundation and final authority of Christian faith as does Scripture.*

4. *We do not believe that the writings of Ellen White may be used as the basis of doctrine. ...*

6. *We do not believe that Scripture can be understood only through the writings of Ellen White*

7. *We do not believe that the writings of Ellen White exhaust the meaning of Scripture..."*

Really? It appears we are faced with something of a contradiction. It's one thing to profess something, but if your actions deny your profession, what is the profession worth? In my experience, in every article, sermon and discussion on the Trinity doctrine, when scriptural references are lacking, the weight of the argument is determined by quotations from Ellen White. For a reminder of the common line of reasoning, just refer back to the quotes from our scholars, Johnson, Valentine, Gane and Knight.

So, we have some hard questions that need honest answers before we can hope to get to the truth of the matter.

So, let us first take a brief look at some of her statements written *after* the writing of *The Desire of Ages,* and see if she did clearly renounce the old non-Trinitarian position. "One thing it is certain is soon to be realized, - the great apostasy, which is developing and increasing and waxing stronger, and will continue to do so until the Lord shall descend from heaven with a shout. We are to hold fast the first principles of our denominated faith, and go forward from the strength to increased faith. Ever we are to keep the faith that has been substantiated by the Holy Spirit of God from the earlier events of our experience until the present time." - *Special Testimonies Series B*, *No.7, p 57.* (1905), *(emphasis supplied).*

"The past fifty years have not dimmed one jot or principle of our faith as we received the great and wonderful evidences that were made certain to us in 1844, after the passing of the time. The languishing souls are to be confirmed and quickened according to His word. And many of the ministers of the gospel and the Lord's physicians will have their languishing souls quickened according to the word. Not a word is changed or denied. That which the Holy Spirit testified to as truth after the passing of the time, in our great disappointment, is the solid foundation of truth. Pillars of truth were revealed, and we accepted the foundation principles that have made us what we are - Seventh-day Adventists, keeping the commandments of God and having the faith of Jesus." - *Special Testimonies Series B, No.7, p 57-58.* (1905) *(Emphasis supplied).*

    From the above two statements we see that the truths that the Pioneers believed have been substantiated by the Holy Spirit to be truth. Ellen White made these statements in 1905, clearly showing that the doctrines that the Pioneers settled upon were the truth, and was unchanged at the time of writing. At no time did she ever state that any of the doctrines of the pioneers in that time period had been incorrect, and needed to be revised. "The past fifty years have not dimmed one jot or principle of our faith," is a clear indication of the time period that she is talking about. The *Declaration of the Fundamental Principles taught and practiced by Seventh-day Adventists* were compiled in 1872 by her husband James White, a practicing non-Trinitarian, and stood during this time period. This Declaration clearly was not a Trinitarian statement of belief.

Two years before this, Ellen White, speaking to the teachers in Emmanuel Missionary College in 1903, stated, "Perilous times are before us. Everyone who has knowledge of the truth should awake, and place himself, body, soul, and spirit, under the discipline of God. Wake up, brethren, wake up. The enemy is on our track. We must be wide awake, on our guard against him. We must put on the whole armor of God. We must follow the directions given in the spirit of prophecy. We must love and obey the truth for this time. This will save us from accepting strong delusions. God has spoken to us through his word. He has spoken to us through the Testimonies to the church, and through the books that have helped to make plain our present duty and the position that we should now occupy. The warnings that have been given, line upon line, precept upon precept, should be heeded. If we disregard them, what excuse shall we offer?"

What was it that Ellen White was warning about? She continued; "The new theories in regard to God and Christ, as brought out in 'The Living Temple', are not in harmony with the teaching of Christ. The Lord Jesus came to this world to represent the Father. He did not represent God as an essence pervading nature, but as a personal being. Christians should bear in mind that God has a personality as verily as has Christ." - SPM p 324. (1903) (Emphasis supplied)

Here we see that Ellen White was warning about "new theories in regard to God and Christ" that were making their way into the church. Repeatedly, Ellen White sounded the warnings not to make God, or Christ, non-entities by blending their personalities. She said in 1905;

"And truly our fellowship is with the Father, and with his Son Jesus Christ. All through the Scriptures, the Father and the Son are spoken of as two distinct personages. You will hear men endeavoring to make the Son of God a nonentity. He and the Father are one, but they are two personages. Wrong sentiments regarding this are coming in, and we shall all have to meet them." – *R & H*. *13-7-1905. (emphasis supplied)*

Ellen White could see that there was a problem. But what was she referring to? What was it we would "all have to meet"? We now know that it entered the Church through the writings of J.H. Kellogg, and it did not end there. The teachings in Kellogg's book "<u>The Living Temple</u>" said Ellen White, was only the 'ALPHA' of the danger, the OMEGA was still to come.

""In the book "<u>Living Temple</u>" there is presented the alpha of deadly heresies. The omega will follow, and will be received by those who are not willing to heed the warning God has given." - *Special Testimonies Series B, No. 2 p50. (Emphasis supplied)*.

What was the *alpha* Ellen White talking about? History tells us that she was talking about Dr. Kellogg's views on the nature of God, which we have come to understand as Pantheism; but was there more to the picture? Interestingly enough, Dr. Kellogg admitted he had become Trinitarian in his thinking; with views on the nature of the Holy Spirit which diverged from those of his contemporaries, and yet, the topic of the "Alpha" is little preached about today. Today it appears we have ignored this warning, and embraced a highly controversial doctrine that, amazingly, is on that very subject, the nature and personality of God, and which the founding Fathers of Adventism condemned in no uncertain manner. It was not until 65 years after her death, at the 1980 General Conference, that the Adventist Church officially became Trinitarian, and all along there were those who opposed it. Without spending more time on the "Alpha" question, which has been dealt with in other books and articles, let us look at a couple of other questions which require answers.

The 1888 Message – a distinctly non-Trinitarian Message.

The Minneapolis General Conference of 1888 is the greatest milestone in Adventist history. Other General Conference Sessions since have been hailed as great, glorious events, but none are still talked about as the 1888 Session. As recorded in the book <u>Christ and His Righteousness</u>, by E J Waggoner, one of the 1888 Messengers endorsed for some years by Ellen White, we find Christ set forth as literally and truly the divine Son of God who was begotten in the recesses of eternity past. Ellen White, God's inspired prophet to

His remnant church, fully endorsed the message of Waggoner and Jones, describing it as a most precious message from God, the Third Angel's message in verity. She enthusiastically endorsed a message which was so decidedly counter to our current teaching on the Trinity! And she believed that if the message had been accepted, it would have resulted in the outpouring of the Latter Rain and shortly thereafter, the second coming of Christ! At the time when we are told the greatest spiritual enlightenment had come to the Church and the world, Ellen White and the leaders were so terribly deluded on this topic (ie. the nature of God) whilst she had everything else correct?

The evidence from history shows that both Waggoner and Jones were non-Trinitarian. Whilst Ellen White was alive, the denominational stance was non-Trinitarian. In fact, Adventists were still opposing Trinitarian concepts coming into the Church well into the 1950's and 60's. Opposition continued from retired pastors, teachers and laymen. But their opposition went unheeded.

Today, it is a minute selection of Ellen White statements which are taken to support the Trinity doctrine, despite the vast number of statements which are clearly non-Trinitarian. If Ellen White taught the Trinity but never used the term, why is it that it can only be deduced with much controversy, especially when she was supposedly making a decided effort to introduce it? When Elder M. L. Andreasen, thinking that the statements in *The Desire of Ages* were a new understanding, visited Ellen White to ascertain if she had indeed penned these words, Mrs. White, although confirming that she had written it, did not in any way link this to the Trinity doctrine. We have no record of the conversation between Ellen White and Andreasen, and he does not tell us if he asked her the specific purpose of her statements in *The Desire of Ages*. This meeting occurred in 1909. It was not until 1948 that we find Andreasen's first public reference to this in a Chapel talk at Loma Linda University. Why did he take so long to comment on it? Is it not strange that she did not embrace an opportune moment to unequivocally state her dramatic change to a new position, particularly in the presence of one of our young up-and-coming Bible teachers of the time?

The Desire of Ages - In *Selected Messages Book I*, p. 296 the same expression as found in *The Desire of Ages* p.530, is used under the caption "Christ the Life Giver". Although this expression is commonly used today to argue that the life of Christ was not begotten, i.e. ingenerate, yet in the same chapter she states that this "life, original, unborrowed and underived" which she describes as immortal life, may also be received as a gift by all repentant sinners. This would be impossible from a Trinitarian understanding. Could it be that we are misunderstanding Ellen White in what she wrote in this much controverted statement?

In the gospel of John we read these words of Christ. "For as the Father hath life in Himself; so hath He given to the Son to have life in Himself; and hath given Him authority to execute judgment also, because He is the Son of man." – John 5:26. This text, which clearly states that Christ was given inherent life by His Father, is in perfect harmony with Ellen White's statement, "life original, unborrowed and underived" but in no way supports the Trinity doctrine. Christ is teaching that He Himself received immortal life from His Father, not as a gift to sinners, but as His inherent birthright as the only begotten Son of God. Hebrews chapter 1 supports this and gives further insight into it.

Ellen White frequently wrote that the Son of God existed from all eternity. She also wrote that He did not always have a separate existence from His Father, which in turn explains his eternal existence. She was equally categorical that he was truly the Son of God, not by creation, not by adoption, but one begotten from the Father's bosom and made in the express image of His Father's person (See *Advent Review & Sabbath Herald*, 07-09-1895; *The Signs of The Times*, 05-30-1895). Again, I find it strange that those who claim that Ellen White taught the Trinity doctrine totally ignore the statements in which she taught the literal pre-incarnate Son ship of Christ?

Between the writing of *The Desire of Ages* in 1898 and 1915, when Ellen White died, although she used several "three" statements in regard to the

Godhead, she never used the term Trinity. Many who claim that these terms, such as "heavenly trio", prove that she taught the Trinity, fail to realize that Ellen White precisely understood what the term "Trinity" meant; one Being with three parts or manifestations functioning as three separate persons, whereas a trio meant three persons or personalities functioning harmoniously to effect one common goal. Could it be that Ellen White was aware that to use the word Trinity would have misrepresented what she believed?

Unlike some in the Church today, she did not believe that 'persons' meant exactly the same as 'beings'. In her writings we find that the term 'being(s)' referred to the Father and the Son who were personal beings. According to the first chapter in <u>Patriarchs and Prophets</u>, the third highest 'being' in Heaven before the entrance of sin, was Lucifer.

Ellen White taught that Christ, the Son of God was a personal, independent being with His own will and self-consciousness as opposed to the established Trinitarian doctrine which teaches that Christ was a *hypostasis* i.e. an expression, mode or extension of the Father. And yet Ellen White is considered to have taught the Trinity when her concept of the Son ship of Christ is fundamentally different. In studying the writings of Ellen White her teachings bear little or no resemblance to the established understanding of the Trinity, and yet many today will argue that her writings support the doctrine.

Is there an answer? So, from all of the above, and without writing another book on the topic, we need to ask ourselves the obvious question. Is there an alternative conclusion we can draw? I would suggest that there is. Could it be that we see our own doctrinal history with pre-conceived vision – glasses darkened with new views that cloud the past? Could it be that Ellen White was in perfect unity with the non-Trinitarian position of her husband and her colleagues; and that there has been a gradual change in *our* understanding on this important doctrine? Could we have reached a point where the facts are made to appear that Ellen White has endorsed this great doctrinal change to the pro-Trinitarian position, when in reality she did not? There is a precedent for this. In Leroy E. Froom's monumental work, "<u>Movement of Destiny</u>", the author spent considerable time attempting to make the 1888 messengers, Waggoner and Jones, appear to be Trinitarian, despite the obvious theological difference in their writings which he conveniently neglected to quote from. Froom's agenda is now well known and an embarrassment to Adventist scholars everywhere. His revisionist history and his work in the Evangelical Conferences of the 1950's left their influence, and a black mark goes down in Adventist history against his name. This information is readily available now, but what did Adventist pastors and laymen believe when his books were first published? As he was regarded as the "official" church historian, his position was generally accepted. Is history being repeated again – today?

In Conclusion- As I have said, the above thoughts and questions demand answers. Since becoming non-Trinitarian in 1993 I have yet to find any Trinitarian who deals with this topic in a satisfactory way. Remember, the Adventist Pioneers had clear doctrinal exegesis for all of our beliefs, and yet when it comes to the Trinity, a very recent addition to the Fundamentals, no one as yet has found one clear text in Scripture to prove the doctrine. By this I mean one text (at least) that shows that God is composed of three co-equal, co-eternal persons or beings; composed of the same substance. Scholars around the world have acknowledged for years that the Trinity doctrine is not found in Scripture but is a later addition. And yet people take sides, arguing theology from a few Ellen White statements, ignoring the word of God, and the vast majority of Ellen White statements over the whole length of her lifetime. She even told us *how* to interpret her writings, but no scholar to date has taken the time to do it. In 1903 she stated: "The testimonies themselves will be the key that will explain the messages given, as scripture is explained by scripture." - <u>1SM</u>, p. 42. She also stated: "He (God) requires of His people faith that rests upon the weight of evidence, not upon perfect knowledge." - <u>3T</u>, p.258

Some have asked; does it really matter which position I take? My personal study has led me to the realization that acceptance of the Trinity doctrine has brought with it a string of other confusing doctrines which grow out of it, the combination of which leads away from the path of truth, into serious error.

The Great Second Advent Movement regarded itself as 'a people of the book'. So does Seventh-day Adventism. No precedent exists for doctrinal change in the history of the Movement where Ellen White was used of God to change the doctrinal direction of the church. For the "Lord has declared that the history of the past shall be rehearsed as we enter upon the closing work. Every truth that He has given for these last days is to be proclaimed to the world. Every pillar that He has established is to be strengthened. We cannot now step off the foundation that God has established." – 2 SM p.390. *(Ms. 129, 1905.)*

If we as a people are to be used by God to restore the Gospel to its original purity, and share it with a world who is dying to hear it, we are faced with a decision. On either side we have the extremes of Arianism and Trinitarianism; - should we not study the word and re-discover the Gospel truth about God, which avoids the pitfalls of both camps, and presents the beauty and simplicity of Christ, the divine Son of God, who came and died, that you and I might choose life, - life, for all eternity. It will take prayer and study on the part of all believers, to re-discover the truth as originally given, that we may be prepared for the true outpouring of the Latter Rain, and not the false.

Let us not forget, "The spirit in which you come to the investigation of the Scriptures *will determine the character of the assistant at your side*. Angels from the world of light will be with those who in humility of heart seek for divine guidance. . . . But if the heart is filled with prejudice, Satan is beside you, and *he will set the plain statements of God's word in a perverted light*." – <u>TM</u>, p.108. (emphasis supplied)

Though this article was long I chose to include it because it clearly shows the battle of this issue and how Satan has brought this attack into God's remnant church. Another website worth reviewing on this issue is http://www.hullquist.com/Bible/bib-onegod-12.htm.

Our SDA church maintains that these pioneers were mistaken when they wrote of the true sonship of Christ to the Father. They say that new light has uncovered their errors. Yet, Ellen White's writings of these men's teachings seem to give a very different picture. We will now look at several of these statements. Some statements may be repeats from above but bear with me because we need a complete picture.

"God has given me light regarding our periodicals. What is it? He has said that the dead are to speak. How? Their works shall follow them. We are to repeat the words of the pioneers in our work, who knew what it cost to search for the truth as for hidden treasure, and who labored to lay the foundation of our work. They moved forward step by step under the influence of the Spirit of God. One by one these pioneers are passing away. The word given me is, <u>Let that which these men have written in the past be reproduced.</u> And in The Signs of the Times let not the articles be long or the print fine. Do not try to crowd everything into one number of the paper. Let the print be good, and let earnest, living experiences be put into the paper... These articles must be reproduced. There is truth and power in them. Men spoke as they were moved by the Holy Spirit.

<u>Let the truths that are the foundation of our faith be kept before the people. Some will depart from the faith, giving heed to seducing spirits and doctrines of devils.</u> They talk science, and the enemy comes in and gives them an abundance of science; but it is not the science of salvation. It is not the science of humility, of consecration, or of the sanctification of the Spirit. We are now to understand what the pillars of our faith are,-the truths that have made us as a people what we are, leading us on step by step." (<u>CW</u> 28.1)

Early Experiences – "After the passing of the time in 1844 we searched for the truth as for hidden treasure. I met with the brethren, and we studied and prayed earnestly. Often we remained together until late at night, and sometimes through the entire night, praying for light and studying the Word. Again and again these brethren came together to study the Bible, in order that they might know its meaning, and be prepared to teach it with power. When they came to the point in their study where they said, "We can do nothing more," the Spirit of the Lord would come upon me. I would be taken off in vision, and a clear explanation of the passages we had been studying would be given me, with instruction as to how we were to labor and teach effectively. Thus light was given that helped us to understand the scriptures in regard to Christ, his mission, and his priesthood. A line of truth extending from that time to the time when we shall enter the city of God, was made plain to me, and I gave to others the instruction that the Lord had given me.

During this whole time I could not understand the reasoning of the brethren. My mind was locked, as it were, and I could not comprehend the meaning of the scriptures we were studying. This was one of the greatest sorrows of my life. I was in this condition of mind until all the principal points of our faith were made clear to our minds, in harmony with the Word of God. The brethren knew that, when not in vision, I could not understand these matters, and they accepted, as light directly from heaven, the revelations given.

Many errors arose, and though I was then little more than a child, I was sent by the Lord from place to place to rebuke those who were holding these false doctrines. There were those who were in danger of going into fanaticism, and I was bidden in the name of the Lord to give them a warning from heaven." 1SM 207

"**In the future, deception of every kind is to arise, and we want solid ground for our feet. We want solid pillars for the building. Not one pin is to be removed from that which the Lord has established.** The enemy will bring in false theories, such as the doctrine that there is no sanctuary. This is one of the points on which there will be a departing from the faith. **Where shall we find safety unless it be in the truths that the Lord has been giving for the last fifty years?**" Ellen White, Advent Review and Sabbath Herald, May 5, 1905

"**Let Pioneers Identify Truth.-When the power of God testifies as to what is truth, that truth is to stand forever as the truth. No after suppositions, contrary to the light God has given are to be entertained.** Men will arise with interpretations of Scripture which are to them truth, but which are not truth. The truth for this time, God has given us as a foundation for our faith. He Himself has taught us what is truth. One will arise, and still another, with new light which contradicts the light that God has given under the demonstration of His Holy Spirit.

A few are still alive who passed through the experience gained in the establishment of this truth. God has graciously spared their lives to repeat and repeat till the close of their lives, the experience through which they passed even as did John the apostle till the very close of his life. And the standard-bearers who have fallen in death, are to speak through the reprinting of their writings. I am instructed that thus their voices are to be heard. They are to bear their testimony as to what constitutes the truth for this time." Ellen White, 1905, <u>Counsels to Writers and Editors</u>, pages 31, 32

  Warnings Against Removing Landmarks – "<u>When men come in who would move one pin or pillar from the foundation which God has established by His Holy Spirit, let the aged men who were pioneers in our work speak plainly, and let those who are dead speak also, by the reprinting of their articles in our periodicals.</u> Gather up the rays of divine light that God has given as He has led His people on step by step in the way of truth. This truth will stand the test of time and trial." <u>1MR</u> 55

  "<u>The Leading points of our faith as we hold them today were firmly established. Point after point was clearly defined, and all the brethren came into harmony. The whole company of believers were united in the truth</u>. There were those who came in with strange doctrines, but we were never afraid to meet them. Our experience was wonderfully established by the revelation of the Holy Spirit." <u>TDG</u> 317

  "Now the Spirit speaketh expressly, that in the latter times some shall depart from the faith, giving heed to seducing spirits, and doctrines of devils; speaking lies in hypocrisy; having their conscience seared with a hot iron." (I Timothy 4:1,2)

"I am instructed that the Lord, by His infinite power, has preserved the right hand of His messenger for more than half a century, in order that the truth, may be written out as He bids me write it for publication, in periodicals and books, Why?- <u>Because if it were not thus written out, when the pioneers in the faith shall die, there would be many, new in the faith, who would sometimes accept as messages of truth teachings that contain erroneous sentiments and dangerous fallacies. Sometimes that which men teach as "special light" is in reality specious error, which, as tares sown among the wheat, will spring up and produce a baleful harvest. And errors of this sort will be entertained by some until the close of this earth's history. There are some, who upon accepting erroneous theories, strive to establish them by collecting from my writings statements of truth, which they use, separated from their proper connection and perverted by association with error.</u> Thus seeds of heresy, springing up and growing rapidly into strong plants, are surrounded by many precious plants of truth, and in this way a mighty effort is made to vindicate the genuineness of the spurious plants.

So it was with the heresies taught in <u>Living Temple</u>. (A BOOK EXPRESSING PANTHEISTIC SENTIMENTS PUBLISHED BY J. H. KELLOGG.) The subtle errors in this book were surrounded by many beautiful truths. ... The seductive fallacies of Satan undermined confidence in the true pillars of the faith, which are grounded on Bible evidence. Truth is sustained by a plain "Thus saith the Lord." But there has been a weaving in of error, and the use of scriptures out of their natural connection, in order to substantiate fallacies, which would deceive, if possible, the very elect. ...

Let not the days pass by and precious opportunities be lost of seeking the Lord with all the heart and mind and soul. If we accept not the truth in the love of it, we may be among the number who will see the miracles wrought by Satan in these last days, and believe them." (Letter 136, April 27, 1906, to Brethren Butler, Daniels, and Irwin. Ellen White, 1906, This Day with God, page 126)

As shown in some of the above statements, the nature of God and this relationship with His Son was directly attacked in the Seventh Day Adventist Church over a hundred years ago in a teaching called Pantheism. Pantheism is basically defined as any religious belief or philosophical doctrine that identifies God with the universe. Simply put, God *is* nature. In his book The Living Temple, Dr. John Harvey Kellogg presented this idea and undermined the true nature of God. Led to its ultimate conclusion in pantheism there is no need of a Savior and the divinity of Christ is attacked. For an in-depth look at this attack the reader should obtain a copy of the book, The Omega Rebellion, by Rick Howard. Here the first lie of Satan began creeping into the church. Pantheism totally denied that Christ existed in the sense that we believed as a people and certainly denied His relationship to His Father.

Ellen White writing of this stated: **"Be not deceived; many will depart from the faith, giving heed to seducing spirits and doctrines of devils. We have now before us the alpha of this danger. The omega will be of a most startling nature. We need to study the words that Christ uttered in the prayer that He offered just before His trial and crucifixion."** <u>1SM</u> 197 This attack on God and His remnant people is but a groundwork that is to lead into the omega rebellion. We will look at this prayer further on, but this prayer identifies the truth of the Father and His Son's relationship not only to each other but how they work together in the heart of the believer for our salvation. Though the alpha of apostasy was resisted and wounded, it did not totally die. The nature of God then came under attack by Rome after Ellen White's death.

This attack is evidenced by the slow, sinister change in the church's doctrinal position over the course of time. Slowly and insidiously the trinity doctrine and all its errors have found their way into the system of belief now professed by our SDA church. Our creed, as evidenced in the book <u>Seventh-day Adventists Believe</u>, now accepts this abominable doctrine. We have accepted a doctrine that our pioneers would not have tolerated. Famous author and Andrews University seminary professor, George Knight, boldly admits this fact in the following statement found in MINISTRY magazine, Oct/1993 p. 10.

"Most of the founders of Seventh-day Adventism would not be able to join the church today if they had to subscribe to the denomination's Fundamental Beliefs." "More specifically, most would not be able to agree to belief number 2, which deals with the doctrine of the Trinity. For Joseph Bates the Trinity was an unscriptural doctrine, for James White it was that 'old Trinitarian absurdity,' and for M.E. Cornell it was a fruit of the great apostasy, along with such false doctrines as Sunday keeping and the immortality of the soul."

"In like manner, most of the founders of Seventh-day Adventism would have trouble with fundamental belief number 4, which holds that Jesus is both eternal and truly God. For J.N. Andrews 'the Son of God...had God for His Father, and did, at some point in the eternity of the past, have beginning of days.' And E.J. Waggoner, of Minneapolis 1888 fame, penned in 1890 that 'there was a time when Christ proceeded forth and came from God...but that time was so far back in the days of eternity that to finite comprehension it is practically without beginning."

"Neither could most of the leading Adventists have agreed with fundamental belief number 5, which implies the person hood of the Holy Spirit. Uriah Smith, for example, not only was anti-Trinitarian and semi-Arian, like so many of his colleagues, but also like them pictured the Holy Spirit as 'that divine mysterious emanation through which They [the Father and the Son] carry forward their great and infinite work.' On another occasion, Smith pictured the Holy Spirit as a 'divine influence' and not a 'person like the Father and the Son."

This should be disturbing to every true SDA believer. Was Ellen White in error when she supported these pioneers or has Satan been busy undermining the basic foundations of the church? Even more disturbing is that a few statements, found in the book <u>Evangelism</u>, are used to try and prove the trinity doctrine. When these statements are not read in the light of all her other writings or in the context of what she was opposing, they seem to contradict everything else her words and actions taught throughout her life. Yet, they are frequently used in just that very way.

The following statement was placed in the book <u>Evangelism</u> and seems to prove that Michael was co-eternal with the Father. **"Christ is the pre-existent, self-existent Son of God.... In speaking of his pre-existence, Christ carries the mind back through dateless ages. He assures us that there never was a time when He was not in close fellowship with the eternal God. He to whose voice the Jews were then listening had been with God as one brought up with Him.--Signs of the Times, Aug. 29, 1900."** <u>Ev 615</u>

It sounds convincing until you look at this statement in the original article she wrote in the "Signs of the Times". The area left out as evidenced by the "...."

is where Ellen White points out the truth of Proverbs chapter 8. Among the omitted material was this quote **"Through Solomon Christ declared: "The Lord possessed Me in the beginning of His way, before His works of old. I was set up from everlasting, from the beginning, or ever the earth was. When there were no depths, I was brought forth; when there were no fountains abounding with water. Before the mountains were settled, before the hills was I brought forth"**

Many of these pro-trinitarianism quotes in the book "Evangelism" seem to have Ellen White making statements that support the idea of three co-eternal and coequal parts of the Godhead. Yet in Patriarchs and Prophets, she clearly states that there was only one being (Christ) that was able to enter into the inner counsels with God. Unless read in context and without omitted text, these would seem to be contradictive in nature. Thus whatever comment she was making, (that was subsequently placed in Evangelism) it was not meant to present the Holy Spirit as being able to enter into the inner counsels of the Father (as a separate entity or independent third part of the Godhead).

Just as a few selected texts in the Bible could easily be used to prove an eternal burning hell (a doctrine that we know to be false), in the same way, certain quotes of Ellen White have been misused to reverse a position that a lifetime of her teachings had established. Yes, Satan has been very busy undermining God's church and, indeed, God's last day prophet as well. He has done over time that which would never have been allowed by a single generation. As a prophet of God, Ellen White should be held to the same standard as other prophets.

The Bible teaches in 2 Peter 1:20: "that *no prophecy of the Scriptures is of any private interpretation*". Any statements by her should be weighed against the other massive wealth of her comments, as well as the Scriptures. A few singled out statements pulled out to prove a point is using the Eisegesis Hermeneutics (reading one's own preconceived ideas into the passage) method of interpreting prophet writings, which we know is an incorrect technique.

So what are we saying? Is this meant to be an attack on the church or its leaders? Absolutely not! Does this mean the church has fallen? Emphatically, it does not! It is only a wake-up call: "THE ENEMY IS UPON US." It is time for God's people to stop feeding on anything but God's word and the Spirit of Prophecy for truth. Study this out in full, prayerfully, and then ask for God's guidance on how to oppose the power of Rome that even now assaults the church. Yes, this is an attack by Satan through Roman Catholicism. It is an attack rooted in the same three lies that Satan deceived mankind with originally. We will see that these have been his consistent method of attacking God's chosen throughout time.

As we saw in Ellen White's comment about the omega of apostasies that is coming: **"We need to study the words that Christ uttered in the prayer that He offered just before His trial and crucifixion.** *"These words spake Jesus, and lifted up his eyes to heaven, and said, Father, the hour is come; glorify thy Son, that thy Son also may glorify thee: as thou hast given him power over all flesh, that he should give eternal life to as many as thou hast given him. And this is life eternal, that they might know thee the only true God, and Jesus Christ, whom thou hast sent. I have glorified thee on the earth: I have finished the work which thou gavest me to do. And now, O Father, glorify thou me with thine own self with the glory which I had with thee before the world was. I have manifested thy name unto the men which thou gavest me out of the world: thine they were, and thou gavest them me; and they have kept thy word* **(John 17:1-6).""** {1SM 197.5}"

One may ask, is the church really in as much danger as this makes it sound? What does the prophet say? **"The warnings of the word of God regarding the perils surrounding the Christian church belong to us today. As in the days of the apostles, men tried by tradition and philosophy to destroy faith in the Scriptures, so today, by the pleasing sentiments of higher criticism, evolution, spiritualism, theosophy, and pantheism, the enemy of righteousness is seeking to lead souls into forbidden paths. To many the Bible is as a lamp without oil, because they have turned their**

minds into channels of speculative belief that bring misunderstanding and confusion. The work of higher criticism, in dissecting, conjecturing, reconstructing, is destroying faith in the Bible as a divine revelation. It is robbing God's word of power to control, uplift, and inspire human lives. By spiritualism, multitudes are taught to believe that desire is the highest law, that license is liberty, and that man is accountable only to himself." (AA 474)

This apostasy is now upon us. Not only has the trinity doctrine attacked the church, but in its God eclipsing shadow, the return of pantheism again threatens us. Spiritualism and occult practices have crept in the back door in the guise of new doctrines called Spiritual Formation and Contemplative (Mystical) (entering the silence) Prayer. These teachings have not only entered our churches but have even infiltrated into our Theological Seminaries, such as Andrews University. We will look at this in much more detail further on in the study of the cross and the sanctuary. If you doubt that this is true, see the following website for an example of this infiltration.

http://www.andrews.edu/sem/dmin/concentrations/discipling/index.html

Ellen White showed that one of the keys to not falling into this last great apostasy is in understanding Christ's great prayer in John 17. It deals with the relationship of the Father to His Son and their relationship to us. In this, we find the great truth of righteousness by faith, the truth that Lucifer hoped you would never find. We will explore it in detail in chapter 10. But first we must follow the great controversy to the next stage. Let's now look back in history to the great battle between Lucifer and Michael at Christ's first advent.

Chapter 6
War in the Wilderness

Nearly 4000 years had passed and as Lucifer looked on the world his thoughts were troubled. The greatest conflict with Michael was soon to take place. He knew that Amos 3:7 states: *"Surely the Lord GOD will do nothing, but he revealeth his secret unto his servants the prophets"*. He knew the Scriptures well and knew, as shown in the prophecies of Daniel, that the time was at hand. He remembered his last two conflicts with Michael and knew that any battle using power alone would be useless.

In Heaven, he and his minions had been overpowered and cast from paradise. Then, after two thousand years, he had corrupted man so badly that Michael had destroyed the world except for Noah and his family who had been saved in the ark. The memory of the event still made him shudder. Never had he seen such destructive power released.

Concerning this event Ellen White wrote: **"As the violence of the storm increased, trees, buildings, rocks, and earth were hurled in every direction. The terror of man and beast was beyond description. Above the roar of the tempest was heard the wailing of a people that had despised the authority of God. Satan himself, who was compelled to remain in the midst of the warring elements, feared for his own existence." PP 99**

Now Satan knew that another great conflict was again to occur between himself and the Son of God. This time his eternal fate would be decided. God had revealed the timing of this to his prophet Daniel. In Daniel 9, he had been shown that there would be a decree issued to rebuild Jerusalem. Christ would then come 483 years later to begin his ministry and then be cut off three and half years later. Artaxerxes, in 457 B.C. at Michael's urging, had made the decree to rebuild Jerusalem and the prophecy's starting point had been established.

Satan had witnessed the birth of Christ right on schedule and had witnessed the proclamation of His birth to the shepherds. He had seen the wise men come from the east to honor and worship the heavenly Sovereign. His hopes that Christ would fail had been raised when he saw how the leaders of God's own chosen people were not looking for Him. Using his power over King Herod, he had tried to have the Child killed. But God had sent an angel warning Joseph of this threat and Christ had escaped.

Thirty years had passed and all attempts to get Jesus to sin or rely upon His own power had failed. Now here was Jesus being baptized in the Jordan River by John the Baptist. *"And Jesus, when he was baptized, went up straightway out of the water: and, lo, <u>the heavens were opened unto him</u>, and he saw the Spirit of God descending like a dove, and lighting upon him: And lo a voice from heaven, saying, <u>This is my beloved Son</u>, in* *whom I am well pleased"* (Matt 3:16-17). Lucifer knew that the waiting time was now over. Over the next 3 ½ years, the war would be decided. The time for the battle to begin was at hand. If he lost this battle, he and his angels' doom was decided for all eternity. He must not allow Jesus to prevail. *"Then was Jesus led up of the Spirit into the wilderness to be tempted of the devil"* (Matt 4:1).

"Satan saw that he must either conquer or be conquered. The issues of the conflict involved too much to be entrusted to his confederate angels. He must personally conduct the warfare. All the energies of apostasy were rallied against the Son of God. Christ was made the mark of every weapon of hell." DA 116.3

It is important to understand the attacks that Satan used in his temptations of Christ. Christ had fasted for forty days and nights and was "anhungred". This is an understatement. After 40 days an individual would literally be close to starving to death. It is at this point that the devil comes to him and says: *"If thou be the Son of God, command that these stones be made bread"* (Matt 4:3).

Christ had not gone out to the wilderness to invite temptation but rather to fast and pray in preparation for His ministry on earth. This ministry was to ultimately lead to His giving up His life for the redemption of mankind. But, after fasting for forty days, Lucifer thought this would be an opportune time for his attack. This is seen in the following statement.

"When Jesus was led into the wilderness to be tempted, He was led by the Spirit of God. He did not invite temptation. He went to the wilderness to be alone, to contemplate His mission and work. By fasting and prayer He was to brace Himself for the bloodstained path He must travel. But Satan knew that the Saviour had gone into the wilderness, and he thought this the best time to approach Him." DA 114

So what was this temptation? Eating bread was not a sin. Bread was part of Christ's regular daily diet. What was the sin that Jesus could commit here? "Weak and emaciated from hunger, worn and haggard with mental agony, "His visage was so marred more than any man, and His form more than the sons of men." Isaiah 52:14. Now was Satan's opportunity. Now he supposed that he could overcome Christ. There came to the Saviour, as if in answer to His prayers, one in the guise of an angel from heaven. He claimed to have a commission from God to declare that Christ's fast was at an end... As God had sent an angel to stay the hand of Abraham from offering Isaac, so, satisfied with Christ's willingness to enter the bloodstained path, the Father had sent an angel to deliver Him; this was the message brought to Jesus. The Saviour was faint from hunger, He was craving for food, when Satan came suddenly upon Him. Pointing to the stones which strewed the desert, and which had the appearance of loaves, the tempter said, "If Thou be the Son of God, command that these stones be made bread."

Though he appears as an angel of light, these first words betray his character. "<u>If Thou be the Son of God.</u>" Here is the insinuation of distrust. Should Jesus do what Satan suggests, it would be an acceptance of the doubt ... "If Thou be the Son of God." The words rankle with bitterness in his mind. In the tones of his voice is an expression of utter incredulity. Would God treat His own Son thus? Would He leave Him in the desert with wild beasts, without food, without companions, without comfort? He insinuates that God never meant His Son to be in such a state as this. "If Thou be the Son of God," show Thy power by relieving Thyself of this pressing hunger. Command that this stone be made bread. The words from heaven, "This is My beloved Son, in whom I am well pleased" (Matthew 3:17), were still sounding in the ears of Satan. But he was determined to make Christ disbelieve this testimony." <u>DA</u> 118

This temptation placed before Jesus had two parts. The first was to disbelieve God when He stated that Jesus was His beloved Son. The second was to try and get Jesus to rely on His own strength. Christ was to be our example so His life was one of continual reliance upon his Father. If ever He had used His own strength instead of strict reliance upon the Father, He could not have been our living example or substitute.

It is an interesting fact that this attack on the relationship of the Father and Son and self-reliance is still being waged today against God's church. Satan still seeks to cause the followers of Christ to doubt this father/son relationship by either demoting Christ from His divinity to that of a created being, or making Him a coeternal deity (more like a brother to the Father) rather than God's actual Son. He also seeks to have us rely on our own strength in trying to keep God's law instead of living the law through righteousness by faith in Christ and His Father.

Christ's defense was found in His faith established in the Father and the knowledge of the Scriptures and their use against Satan. It is the same and only effective defense that we can use against the devil's attacks today. Christ said: *"It is written, Man shall not live by bread alone, but by every word that proceedeth out of the mouth of God."* (Matthew 4:4)

For those of the remnant living in the last days of earth's history, this answer is very important. His answer of "every word" has significant implications for God's remnant church. God, in His mercy and wisdom, blessed the remnant church with the Spirit of Prophecy. In the gift of a prophet (Ellen White) to His church, God has given us the information and warnings needed to combat Satan in his final assault on the church. That is why we have seen such a concerted effort on Satan's part to attack the validity of God's last day prophet. "Every word" would certainly include His last day prophet.

Ellen White was shown by inspiration that this attack would occur and gave dire warnings in the following several statements. When read collectively, they should give any SDA member cause to pause and consider their spiritual significance in choosing whether to heed God's messenger or not.

"Do we believe that we are coming to the crisis, that we are living in the very last scenes of the earth's history? Will we now awaken and do the work which this time calls for, or will we wait till the things which I have presented come upon us? ... And this witness Satan will strive most earnestly to silence, that he may better obtain access to minds by making of none effect the testimonies of the Spirit of God." 1SAT 91

"The word of God is not silent in regard to this momentous time, determining not to hear, not to receive, not to obey. The Lord's messages of light have been before us for years, but there have been influences working indirectly to make of none effect the warnings coming through the Sentinel and the "Testimonies" {RH, December 18, 1888 par. 6 Ellen G White}

"It was the spirit of Satan expressed in looks and words to make of none effect the Testimonies of the Spirit of God. "This," said the guide with me, "is the way any message of Heaven will be treated."" PH155

"Satan's purpose is, through his devices, to make of none effect the testimonies of the Spirit of God. If he can lead the minds of the people of God to see things in a perverted light, they will lose confidence in the messages God sends through His servants; then he can the more readily deceive, and not be detected." 12MR 201

"Very adroitly some have been working to make of no effect the Testimonies of warning and reproof that have stood the test for half a century. At the same time, they deny doing any such thing." SpTA12

"**The very last deception of Satan will be to make of none effect the testimony of the Spirit of God. "Where there is no vision, the people perish."** Proverbs 29:18. Satan will work ingeniously, in different ways and through different agencies, to unsettle the confidence of God's remnant people in the true testimony." FLB 296

"It is Satan's plan to weaken the faith of God's people in the Testimonies. <u>Next follows skepticism in regard to the vital points of our faith, the pillars of our position</u>, then doubt as to the Holy Scriptures, and then the downward march to perdition. When the Testimonies, which were once believed, are doubted and given up, Satan knows the deceived ones will not stop at this; <u>and he redoubles his efforts till he launches them into open rebellion, which becomes incurable and ends in destruction.</u>" 4T 211

In the Spirit of Prophecy, we are warned of an omega [last] apostasy that would shake the remnant church to its foundation. It was so sinister that Ellen White stated it made her tremble for the church. In the last of the statements listed above, we see that it correlates to making of none effect the testimonies given by God to prepare His remnant church for this very final attack.

As an SDA member we should be asking ourselves one question. Have we read the 9 volumes of <u>Testimonies for the Church</u>? Not just used them for the occasional reference to eisogesisly prove a point but actually read them with an open mind (exegesisly).

When Satan saw that he had been unsuccessful in his first attempt to tempt Christ to sin, he then changed the method of his assault. Using his first temptation, he had been unable to shake the faith of Jesus in His relationship with the Father and His dependence upon Him. **"Then the devil taketh Him up into the holy city, and setteth Him on a pinnacle of the temple, and saith unto Him, If Thou be the Son of God, cast Thyself down: for it is written, He shall give His angels charge concerning Thee: And in their hands they shall bear Thee up, Lest at any time Thou dash Thy foot against a stone ... The tempter thought to take advantage of Christ's humanity, and urge Him to presumption. But while Satan can solicit, he cannot compel to sin. He said to Jesus, "Cast Thyself down," knowing that he could not cast Him down; for God would interpose to deliver Him. Nor could Satan force Jesus to cast Himself down. Unless Christ should consent to temptation, He could not be overcome. Not all the power of earth or hell**

could force Him in the slightest degree to depart from the will of His Father." DA 124,125

Notice that again Satan tried to tempt Christ to doubt His relationship with His Father. But this time Satan also used the word of God to try and tempt Christ into the sin of presumption. He tried to access pride in Christ's human nature by making Christ feel the need to prove His belief that He was the Son of God.

Therefore, we see that although the approach was different, the temptation's ultimate goal was the same - doubt His relationship as true Son of the Father, and reliance on self this time to try and force God's hand. This time Satan misused the Scriptures or changed their context in order to try and deceive Christ. The same attack is again used against God's church today. Like Christ, our defense is found in knowledge of the Scriptures.

"Jesus declared to Satan, "It is written again, Thou shalt not tempt the Lord thy God." These words were spoken by Moses to the children of Israel when they thirsted in the desert, and demanded that Moses should give them water, exclaiming, "Is the Lord among us, or not?" Exodus 17:7. God had wrought marvelously for them; yet in trouble they doubted Him, and demanded evidence that He was with them. In their unbelief they sought to put Him to the test. And Satan was urging Christ to do the same thing. God had already testified that Jesus was His Son; and now to ask for proof that He was the Son of God would be putting

God's word to the test,--tempting Him. And the same would be true of asking for that which God had not promised. It would manifest distrust, and be really proving, or tempting, Him. We should not present our petitions to God to prove whether He will fulfill His word, but because He will fulfill it; not to prove that He loves us, but because He loves us. "Without faith it is impossible to please Him: for he that cometh to God must believe that He is, and that He is a rewarder of them that diligently seek Him." Hebrews 11:6. ...

Often when Satan has failed of exciting distrust, he succeeds in leading us to presumption. If he can cause us to place ourselves unnecessarily in the way of temptation, he knows that the victory is his. God will preserve all who walk in the path of obedience; but to depart from it is to venture on Satan's ground. There we are sure to fall. The Saviour has bidden us, "Watch ye and pray, lest ye enter into temptation." Mark 14:38. Meditation and prayer would keep us from rushing unbidden into the way of danger, and thus we should be saved from many a defeat." DA 126

In this second attack came the temptation to require proof from God. This is rooted in Satan's second lie to Eve where he tempted Eve to believe she needed further enlightenment rather than to simply trust in God based upon his word alone. Simple faith isn't enough, he claimed, you need further enlightenment. He suggests the same to us today. It is not enough to know and believe God by faith alone. We must become enlightened, thus providing proof that what God says is really true. Jesus was not fooled then, and neither should we be now.

At this point Lucifer began to realize that he could not deceive Christ and made a direct frontal assault no longer trying to disguise himself. He flatly offered Jesus the same temptation. You don't need to die, he stated. This mission where your Father is giving you up to die is not necessary. You can be free of God the Father and have all the kingdoms of the world. This was an offer of an exalted position compared to the humble life and death that Christ was to walk. You can be like God being the ruler of the entire world. You will have an elevated and enlightened view of the world and the power over it; only worship me. Through self-exaltation, it can all be yours. Through me, Satan tempts, you can be as God having all and knowing good and evil. Yet, again, Christ's response was the same. *"It is written."*

Satan had lost. His hatred surged, but he was forced to leave Christ for a while as angels attended to their Creator. Christ had been victorious by His choice to hold on by faith to the belief that He was the true Son of God and to rely totally on His Father for strength. He did not seek further enlightenment or a higher state of existence but held on to the established word of God and His faith in His Father. He chose humility over pride and exaltation.

Chapter 7
Victory in the Garden

Now as Christ set out on His ministry, Satan sought to prevent the truth of Christ's mission to reach humanity. Satan, in his lie to humanity, had offered a supposed enlightenment of being like the Most High. It is interesting that this lie was a twisted version of the truth which Christ was to offer mankind.

Jesus came into the world to present a truth that man should not exalt himself but instead die to self. He taught that if a man is reborn of water and of the spirit, the mind (character) of His Father will be given freely to that man. The heart of the gospel is that the sanctifying presence of Jesus will change our minds to be like His. Thus, the truly enlightened mind is filled with the presence of Jesus and the Father changing our characters into their image, thus, changing our very nature.

"Let this mind be in you, which was also in Christ Jesus." (Philippians 2:5) Jesus speaking to His disciples stated: *"At that day ye shall know that I am in my Father, and ye in me, and I in you. He that hath my commandments, and keepeth them, he it is that loveth me: and he that loveth me shall be loved of my Father, and I will love him, and will manifest myself to him."* (John 14:20-21) Later, in Christ's prayer to His Father, He prayed concerning us: *"That they all may be one; as*

thou, Father, art in me, and I in thee, that they also may be one in us: that the world may believe that thou hast sent me. And the glory which thou gavest me I have given them; that they may be one, even as we are one: I in them, and thou in me, that they may be made perfect in one; and that the world may know that thou hast sent me, and hast loved them, as thou hast loved me." (John 17:21-23)

His promise is that by beholding Him we become changed. "**Those who make Christ their daily companion and familiar friend will feel that the powers of an unseen world are all around them; and by looking unto Jesus they will become assimilated to His image. By beholding they become changed to the divine pattern; their character is softened, refined, and ennobled for the heavenly kingdom.**" 4T 616

This principle was taught throughout His ministry here on earth. We will not spend a lot of time on the specifics of His life. The author highly recommends the book Desire of Ages by Ellen G. White. It is my considered opinion that no other book has ever been penned that even comes close to revealing the true life of Christ in all its fullness and love. To sum it up, His life ever reflected the character of His Father and His selfless love for mankind.

We will now move forward to the point where Satan was to make his last stand in trying to defeat Christ in His plan for man's redemption. It was in the Garden of Gethsemane where Lucifer, the prince of this world, would be victorious or be cast down. It is true that at the cross Lucifer was forever defeated but it was in the garden that Christ would be victorious or be defeated.

"In the wilderness of temptation the destiny of the human race had been at stake. Christ was then conqueror. Now the tempter had come for the last fearful struggle. For this he had been preparing during the three years of Christ's ministry. Everything was at stake with him. If he failed here, his hope of mastery was lost; the kingdoms of the world would finally become Christ's; he himself would be overthrown and cast out. But if Christ could be overcome, the earth would become Satan's kingdom, and the human race would be forever in his power." CSA 32

"Here the mysterious cup trembled in His (Christ's) hand. Here the destiny of a lost world was hanging in the balance. Should He wipe the blood drops from His brow and root from His soul the guilt of a perishing world, which was placing Him, all innocent, all undeserving, under the penalty of a just law? Should He refuse to become sinners' substitute and surety? Refuse to give them another trial, another probation? Separation from His Father, the punishment for transgression and sin, was to fall upon Him in order to magnify God's law and testify to its immutability. And this was to settle forever the controversy between the Prince of God and Satan in regard to the changeless character of that law. The Majesty of heaven was as one bewildered with agony." <u>CTr</u> 266

In the garden the weight of the sins of the world was slowly being laid on Christ. The weight of these sins began to crush His life away. At the same time the Father's presence, which Jesus had known continually since the beginning, began to be withdrawn from Him. The One, who had for ages been His Loving Father, His closest Friend, and in whose love and delight he had ever basked since His birth in the eons of time past, was now rejecting Him. The mental anguish He suffered is beyond our understanding. He began to sweat great drops of blood (Hematidrosis) as the stress began to overwhelm His physical strength. In anguish, He prayed: *"O my Father, if it be possible, let this cup pass from me: nevertheless not as I will, but as thou wilt."* (Matthew 26:30) Lucifer sees that the Father is withdrawing from Christ and that this separation threatens to overwhelm Him. It is now that Satan presses his attack.

"The gulf was so broad, so black, so deep, that His spirit shuddered before it. This agony He must not exert His divine power to escape. As man He must suffer the consequences of man's sin. As man He must endure the wrath of God against transgression.

Christ was now standing in a different attitude from that in which He had ever stood before. His suffering can best be described in the words of the prophet, "*Awake, O sword, against My shepherd, and against the man that is My fellow, saith the Lord of hosts.*" Zechariah 13:7. As the substitute and surety for sinful man, Christ was suffering under divine justice. He saw what justice meant. Hitherto He had been as an intercessor for others; now He longed to have an intercessor for Himself.

As Christ felt His unity with the Father broken up, He feared that in His human nature He would be unable to endure the coming conflict with the powers of darkness. In the wilderness of temptation the destiny of the human race had been at stake. Christ was then conqueror. Now the tempter had come for the last fearful struggle. For this he had been preparing during the three years of Christ's ministry. Everything was at stake with him. If he failed here, his hope of mastery was lost; the kingdoms of the world would finally become Christ's; he himself would be overthrown and cast out. But if Christ could be overcome, the earth would become Satan's kingdom, and the human race would be forever in his power. With the issues of the conflict before Him, Christ's soul was filled with dread of separation from God. Satan told Him that if He became the surety for a sinful world, the separation would be eternal. He would be identified with Satan's kingdom, and would nevermore be one with God.

And what was to be gained by this sacrifice? How hopeless appeared the guilt and ingratitude of men! In its hardest features Satan pressed the situation upon the Redeemer: The people who claim to be above all others in temporal and spiritual advantages have rejected You. They are seeking to destroy You, the foundation, the center and seal of the promises made to them as a peculiar people. One of Your own disciples, who has listened to Your instruction, and has been among the foremost in church activities, will betray You. One of Your most zealous followers will deny You. All will forsake You. Christ's whole being abhorred the thought. That those whom He had undertaken to save, those whom He loved so much, should unite in the plots of Satan, this pierced His soul. The conflict was terrible. Its measure was the guilt of His nation, of His accusers and betrayer, the guilt of a world lying in wickedness. The sins of men weighed heavily upon Christ, and the sense of God's wrath against sin was crushing out His life.** DA 687

In this last battle, Satan sought to have Jesus base His decisions on the evidence before Him. He pressed that if Jesus was to sacrifice His life that it would be for nothing. His relationship with His Father, which must now be based on faith alone, was again brought under fire. Satan told Jesus that if He was to take our sins upon Himself the He would forever belong to him. He urged that this separation was beyond that which the Father could work out and would be eternal. Even further, he urged that it was all for nothing, that no one cared about the sacrifice He was making. **"How dark seemed the malignity of sin! Terrible was the temptation to let the human race bear the consequences of its own guilt,** while He stood innocent before God. If He could only know that His disciples understood and appreciated this, He would be strengthened. Rising with painful effort, He staggered to the place where He had left His companions. But He "findeth them asleep." DA 687

This happened twice and upon the third time He returned to the same place and again fell praying to God as the great darkness of sin settled more fully upon him. Finally, the humanity in Him could bear no more. The weight of sin was actually crushing Him as death threatened to take Him. With His last strength He groaned: *"saying, O my Father, if this cup may not pass away from me, except I drink it, thy will be done."* (Matthew 26:42)

"Having made the decision, He fell dying to the ground from which He had partially risen. Where now were His disciples, to place their hands tenderly beneath the head of their fainting Master, and bathe that brow, marred indeed more than the sons of men? The Saviour trod the wine press alone, and of the people there was none with Him.

But God suffered with His Son. Angels beheld the Saviour's agony. They saw their Lord enclosed by legions of satanic forces, His nature weighed down with a shuddering, mysterious dread. There was silence in heaven ... the mighty angel who stands in God's presence, occupying the position from which Satan fell, came to the side of Christ. The angel came not to take the cup from Christ's hand, but to strengthen Him to

drink it, with the assurance of the Father's love. He came to give power to the divine-human suppliant. He pointed Him to the open heavens, telling Him of the souls that would be saved as the result of His sufferings. He assured Him that His Father is greater and more powerful than Satan, that His death would result in the utter discomfiture of Satan, and that the kingdom of this world would be given to the saints of the Most High." DA 693

Praise and glory be to our Savior. He had been victorious. Though the terrible events that were to lead up to His crucifixion were still before Him, He had won the battle. Satan would unleash all the cruelty and malice of his malignant hatred upon his Creator, but it would be in vain. In both points, Christ had remained faithful. He never doubted or sinned in regard to His status as being the true Son of God; and thus He relied fully upon the strength of His heavenly Father and never upon His own strength. Even more, He demonstrated the selfless love of God's character by taking our death penalty upon Himself to pay the penalty for our sin of treason.

In His victory, Jesus became not only the lamb sacrificed for our sins by His death, but also He became our example by His life. The lie that Satan offered our parents of being raised into a higher state was now to meet its true counterpart. Christ showed us that through a life of humility and self-sacrifice in Him we might be lifted up as adopted sons of God. *"Submit yourselves* therefore to God. Resist the devil, and he will flee from you. Draw nigh to God, and he will draw nigh to you. Cleanse your hands, ye sinners; and purify your hearts, ye double minded. Be afflicted, and mourn, and weep: let your laughter be turned to mourning, and your joy to heaviness. Humble yourselves in the sight of the Lord, and he shall lift you up." (James 4:7-10)

"Behold, what manner of love the Father hath bestowed upon us, that we should be called the sons of God: therefore the world knoweth us not, because it knew him not. Beloved, now are we the sons of God, and it doth not yet appear what we shall be: but we know that, when he shall appear, we shall be like him; for we shall see him as he is." (1 John 3:1-2)

"In the contemplation of Christ we linger on the shore of a love that is measureless. We endeavor to tell of this love, and language fails us. We consider His life on earth, His sacrifice for us, His work in heaven as our advocate, and the mansions He is preparing for those who love Him, and we can only exclaim, O the height and depth of the love of Christ! "Herein is love, not that we loved God, but that He loved us, and sent His Son to be the propitiation for our sins." "*Behold, what manner of love the Father hath bestowed upon us, that we should be called the sons of God*." 1 John 4:10; 3:1." AA 333

Chapter 8
Three Unclean Spirits

As I begin this chapter I want to go on record as stating that I fully accept the truths of the sanctuary as we have been given them as the Advent people. This chapter, however, will go into a deeper look at the cross and its truths that have lain hidden in the sanctuary of ancient Israel. For those who have not studied the sanctuary doctrine this may seem a little daunting, but you will see the plain truths of the cross within its walls. You may be wondering why we are going back in history to a time hundreds of years prior to Christ's death to look at an Old Testament ritualistic system of worship. The truth is that the sanctuary and its system of sacrifices was the type that met its antitype in the cross of Christ.

This truth is fundamental to our understanding of Christ's death for our sins on that cross. This is brought to light in the Biblical reference to Christ as the Lamb of God. It is further seen when *"... John (the Baptist) seeth Jesus coming unto him, and saith, Behold the Lamb of God, which taketh away the sin of the world."* (John 1:29) In fact, John the disciple refers to Him as the Lamb slain from the foundation of the world. (Revelation 13:8) **"Paul showed how closely God had linked the sacrificial service with the prophecies relating to the One who was to be "brought as a lamb to the slaughter." The**

Messiah was to give His life as "an offering for sin." Looking down through the centuries to the scenes of the Saviour's atonement, the prophet Isaiah had testified that the Lamb of God "poured out His soul unto death: and He was numbered with the transgressors; and He bare the sin of many, and made intercession for the transgressors." Isaiah 53:7, 10, 12. AA 227

After Christ's victory in the garden, He was taken before the Jewish leaders, to Pilot, to Herod, back to Pilot, being mocked and tortured at each stop and along the way. He was finally delivered up to be crucified after being scourged twice. The pain and suffering that Satan brought to bear upon Him was the most severe Satan's heart of malice could heap upon Christ. The question for fallen man then becomes, why? Why would the Father allow His Son to suffer such horrors wrought by Satan's malevolence? Why would Jesus allow Himself to suffer this indignation and abject cruelty? What did Christ fully achieve at the cross?

Christ stated: *"And I, if I be lifted up from the earth, will draw all men unto me."* (John 12:32) What does this mean? What we will find is that He not only paid for the sins of fallen man, not only lived the perfect life as our righteous example and substitute, but He also gave a revelation of the infinite and boundless love of the Father for fallen sinners. Christ, as the Lamb of God, became the source of salvation to all of mankind. Whosoever looks to Him, no matter what fallen system they find themselves bound, will be freed from sin and its taskmaster. Jesus also became the ultimate source of refuge for His faithful servants as revealed in the sanctuary of ancient Israel.

But first, we must look closer at each of the fallen systems of worship that exist today. We will also look at Satan's subtle attacks from each system on God's remnant church. Only then can we see the deeper truths of the cross for our time and spread the good news of the gospel (as seen in the third angel's message) to a fallen world.

In the world today there are three major categories or systems of religion that are at enmity with Christ and thus also at enmity with His remnant Church. They have each fallen to three distinct doctrines from the evil one. With these doctrines, they resist the power of the cross and attack its truth. We will look at these doctrines and the systems of worship more closely. They all have something in common. They all attack the relationship and character of Jesus and His Father in three unique ways. These religious systems are:

1. The Dragon - Paganism – Hinduism, Buddhism, Taoism, Witchcraft, New Age, Druidism, etc.
2. The Beast – Catholicism/Fallen Christianity – Babylon and her Daughters (Revelation 17:5)
3. The False Prophet - Islam – Muhammad - and the Twelver's 12th Imam (Revelation 16:13, 2 John 1:7)

In Revelation 16:13-14 we read: *"And I saw three unclean spirits like frogs come out of the mouth of the dragon, and out of the mouth of the beast, and out of the mouth of the false prophet. For they are the spirits of devils, working miracles, which go forth unto the kings of the earth and of the whole world, to gather them to the battle of that great day of God Almighty."*

Let's begin with an examination of how each system attacks Jesus and the truth of the cross in their doctrines. Look at the above text carefully. Note that each system has all three unclean spirits. The text does not say that each has an unclean spirit but that all three unclean spirits are coming out of the mouth (teachings) of each system.

At this point some who are Bible and prophecy students will no doubt say "wait". They will identify the false prophet with apostate Protestantism, and this book is not denying that an application of this prophecy in that light is correct. But the Scriptures and inspiration reveal another deeper fulfillment of this prophecy that is being fulfilled at this last stage in earth's history. Have you ever wondered why the largest religion in the world would be seemingly left out of the prophecies of warning for God's end time people? Islam has, in fact, not been left out at all as we will see in the coming pages.

First, we must examine the dragon. Who is the dragon and who worships him? The question of who constitutes the dragon is clearly answered in the

Scriptures. *"And he laid hold on the dragon, that old serpent, which is the Devil, and Satan, and bound him a thousand years."* (Revelation 20:2) Unmistakably, the Bible shows that the dragon is Satan (Lucifer).

Identifying his followers or systems that worship him is mostly straightforward as well. The church of Satan boldly proclaims it openly. Free Masonry and other secret societies seek to hide it from their lower members (goyim); but the higher members of their order worship him by name. Others give Lucifer different names such as The Cosmic Christ, Maitreya, and Jampa. In pagan religions, he has been known as Baal, Osiris, and Shiva just to name a few.

They believe the lie that we become as gods through enlightenment and spiritual exercises. This is also seen in many of the eastern religions where dragon images are the central figure in many, if not most of them. The yin yang is a symbol of this enlightenment and higher plane of existence, thus knowing (being one with) both good and evil. We will look at this doctrine in more detail in the following pages. Many of these dragon and heathen religions can trace their roots back to Egypt. The common Egyptian worshipped Isis, Osiris, and Horus in sun, moon, and star worship. Buried within this practice was a deeper knowledge, held by the Egyptian occultist priests, where Lucifer (as the deity within the star of Sirius) was worshipped.

"As we near the close of time, there will be greater and still greater external parade of heathen power;

heathen deities will manifest their signal power, and will exhibit themselves before the cities of the world; and this delineation has already begun to be fulfilled. " EV 705.1

As prophesied, we see a large movement in the world today pulling these religions together into a singular new age philosophy. Meditation, self-empowerment and enlightenment are central themes. In these meditations for spiritual enlightenment, people learn to use meditation and spiritual exercises such as yoga to silence the mind.

With the mind's protection down, in time and often in the form of "spirit guides", Satan and his angels take over the mind leading men farther and farther from God into the depths of spiritualism. Often those mesmerized by Satan experience what they believe to be past life experiences, astral projection, and even converse with dead from the past.

"It is fondly supposed that heathen superstitions have disappeared before the civilization of the twentieth century. But the word of God and the stern testimony of facts declare that sorcery is practiced in this age as verily as in the days of the old-time magicians. The ancient system of magic is, in reality, the same as what is now known as modern spiritualism. Satan is finding access to thousands of minds by presenting himself under the guise of departed friends. The Scriptures declare that "the dead know not anything." Ecclesiastes 9:5. Their thoughts,

their love, their hatred, have perished. The dead do not hold communion with the living. But true to his early cunning, Satan employs this device in order to gain control of minds. Through spiritualism many of the sick, the bereaved, the curious, are communicating with evil spirits. All who venture to do this are on dangerous ground." AA 289

The entrapped are led into believing that they are becoming one with the divine. This form of new age spirituality and philosophy is growing fast. Its influence is vast as seen in its subtle yet steady infiltration into western culture. On the internet website www.amazingdiscoveries.org, there is a lecture available by Professor Walter Veith called the New Age Agenda. I highly recommend this DVD. It has extensive material on this very subject.

In this first great apostate religion, three unclean doctrines are seen coming from its mouth (teachings). Their teachings are:

1. They deny that Christ is the Son of God. They either deny His existence totally or they see Him as an individual who became enlightened and was elevated into the oneness with the divine. He thus becomes equal to Buddha and other great gurus in joining the great cosmic energy matrix pattern that forms God. The soul is immortal and part of this energy matrix, and thus they will not surely die being part of

God. They either pass on into the energy god matrix or, if they choose, they can be reincarnated after death.

2. They are saved by their works through mastering education, empowerment, spiritual exercises, and enlightenment. This is done through meditative practices, such as mantras and meditating on a flame to silence the mind. This is commonly known as Spiritual Formation or Contemplative (Mystical) Prayer. Reliance on reason through self-empowerment is essential (become the god or goddess of reason).

3. As the mind becomes enlightened, they experience Kundalini where energy coiled at the base of the spine like a serpent is released and travels up through the chakra energy centers in the body elevating them into a state of oneness with the divine in the quiet temple of their mind. There they are often led by spirit guides (often supposed dead loved ones or past life friends) thus becoming one with the God–Energy-Matrix. In this oneness, they can experience supernatural states such as past life experiences and astral projection. One may even develop abilities such as levitation. It is believed that God exists in every living thing and a realization is gained that they are part

of God. Pantheism, in short, is alive and doing very well.

It can be seen under this set of doctrines or beliefs that there is no such thing as sin, and there is no need of a Savior. Therefore, Jesus is not God's Son slain from the foundation of the world. **"These theories, followed to their logical conclusion, sweep away the whole Christian economy. They do away with the necessity for the atonement and make man his own savior. These theories regarding God make His word of no effect..."** CCh 323

Remember that in these doctrines it is taught that everyone, through effective meditation into the silence and effectual use of reason, can be as gods. Notice that the same three part lie given to our first parents still exists.

1. There is no true Son of God. Therefore, there is no need of the Father/Son Spirit of God. Man will surely not die because his soul is immortal.
2. Through his own strength, enlightenment can be obtained.
3. Empowered through enlightenment, he will become like God knowing both good and evil and enter a higher state of existence.

The foul, unclean spirits coming out of the mouth of the dragon also come out of the mouth of the second great apostate religion known as the Beast. This beast was seen by Daniel and John rising out of the sea.

"After this I saw in the night visions, and behold a fourth beast, dreadful and terrible, and strong exceedingly; and it had great iron teeth: it devoured and brake in pieces, and stamped the residue with the feet of it: and it was diverse from all the beasts that were before it; and it had ten horns." (Dan 7:7) *"And I stood upon the sand of the sea, and saw a beast rise up out of the sea, having seven heads and ten horns, and upon his horns ten crowns, and upon his heads the name of blasphemy."* (Revelation 13:1)

Historically, this beast has been identified as the Roman Empire. As the Empire of Rome became separated into its 10 kingdoms in AD 476, it was represented by the ten horns on the beast's head. In prophecy, horns always represent kingdoms. But in the prophecy, three of these kingdoms were rooted up and fell to a new evolving little horn kingdom or power. History shows that the Heruli, Vandals, and the Ostrogoths fell as predicted to this new rising power. *"I considered the horns, and, behold, there came up among them another little horn, before whom there were three of the first horns plucked up by the roots: and, behold, in this horn were eyes like the eyes of man, and a mouth speaking great things."* (Daniel 7:8)

This power was different from the other powers in that it was religious/political in nature. *"And the ten horns out of this kingdom are ten kings that shall arise: and another shall rise after them; and he shall be diverse from the first, and he shall subdue three kings. And he shall speak great words against the most High, and shall wear out the saints of the most High, and think to change times and laws: and they shall be given into his hand until a time and times and the dividing of time."* (Daniel 7:24-25) Again, this was fulfilled with the fall of the Heruli, Vandals, and the Ostrogoths. All of this could have been fulfilled by only one entity, the Papacy. In AD 533, Justinian set a decree that the Bishop of Rome (the Pope) was to be the supreme ruler of the churches but this could not be completed until those opposed to the Papacy (specifically the Heruli, Vandals, and the Ostrogoths) were overthrown. This was accomplished by AD 538. This little horn power (the Papacy) would then rule supreme for 1260 years. This is what the time, times and dividing of times represented in Daniel's text above.

It is also seen in the following: *"And I heard the man clothed in linen, which was upon the waters of the river, when he held up his right hand and his left hand unto heaven, and sware by him that liveth for ever that it shall be for a time, times, and an half; and when he shall have accomplished to scatter the power of the holy people, all these things shall be finished."* (Daniel 12:7)

In the book of Revelation, it is seen in the follow text: *"And the woman fled into the wilderness, where she hath a place prepared of God, that they should feed her there a thousand two hundred and threescore days."* (Revelation 12:6)

There are other references, but the point has been made. If Papal Rome is the beast, then 1260 years from AD 538 there would be an event that would end this supremacy. Exactly on schedule, in the year of 1798, the Roman Papal Church fell to the French Armies under the command of General Louis Alexandre Berthier. The Pope was taken captive and later died in exile. This wound to the Papacy was foretold in prophecy.

But if Rome, who today is growing in power, is that beast power then that wound would have to heal. In fact, its wound would have to fully heal because the teachings and doctrines of the Papacy are seen in almost all of the Christian churches today. There was a period of reformation in the church headed up by men like Martin Luther, John Huss, and John Wesley that protested the corruption and paganism in the Papacy. But the Protestant churches, which resulted from these reformer's teachings, have today renewed their ties to Rome and are now again following after her teachings.

Was this deadly wound which healed and the subsequent following after Papal Rome by Christianity foreseen in the Scriptures? *"And I saw one of his heads as it were wounded to death; and his deadly wound was healed: and all the world wondered after the beast."* (Revelation 13:3)

Another identifying sign of this little horn power of the beast was that it would think to change God's times and laws. This is seen clearly in how the Papacy removed the second commandment of God's Decalogue allowing idolatry into the church. The Papacy also changed God's holy Sabbath of the fourth commandment from Saturday to Sunday (venerable day of the sun). Thus, the only commandment of God with His identifying signature as man's Creator and rightful Lord was removed.

"And he shall speak great words against the most High, and shall wear out the saints of the most High, and think to change times and laws: and they shall be given into his hand until a time and times and the dividing of time" (Daniel 7:25) The Papacy did make war on the saints, and those who opposed her were burned at the stake. She was the power behind the Spanish inquisition, thus, persecuting (wearing out) the saints of God. Rome's atrocities, towards God's church in the wilderness (the Waldenses and those like them), are well documented.

The evidence is overwhelming that the Papacy is that very beast power foretold in prophecy. *"So he carried me away in the spirit into the wilderness: and I saw a woman sit upon a scarlet coloured beast, full of names of blasphemy, having seven heads and ten horns. And the woman was arrayed in purple and scarlet colour, and decked with gold and precious stones and pearls, having a golden cup in her hand full of abominations and filthiness of her fornication: And upon her forehead was a name written, MYSTERY, BABYLON THE GREAT, THE MOTHER OF HARLOTS AND ABOMINATIONS OF THE EARTH. And I saw the woman drunken with the blood of the saints, and with the blood of the martyrs of Jesus:* (Daniel 7:25)

This has just touched the surface of this great truth concerning the beast power of Daniel and Revelation. For a complete series of lectures on this subject with overwhelming evidence, I again recommend the website www.amazingdiscoveries.org. On that sight you will find a complete series of DVD's available entitled <u>Total Onslaught</u>. I highly recommend them, if you have any doubt as to this truth.

What is interesting in the above text is that this woman who always represents a church in prophecy is a harlot and is the mother of harlots. Rome is the mother of harlots. Apostate Protestantism (those who follow her doctrines) is her daughter. All are impure thus being represented as harlots. They are not faithful to Jesus and thus not His bride. Hence, they are all represented, as a group, as apostate Christianity.

Now let's review Revelation 16:13 again where we read: *"And I saw three unclean spirits like frogs come out of the mouth of the dragon, and out of the mouth of the beast, and out of the mouth of the false prophet. "* We will now view these three unclean spirits as seen in the doctrines of Rome and apostate Protestantism.

> 1. They deny that Christ is the true Son of God. They either see Him as an eternal generation or procession from the Father or as a co-equal (like Brother) to the Father. Man is also

presented as having an immortal soul and thus they cannot (or they surely will not) die. This doctrine is also furthered in a belief that man can continue to sin and not die. It denies God's sanctifying power in the life. Man also can come to God through Mary and other saints. This again denies the Father/Son relationship essentiality in our salvation as seen in the prayer of John chapter seventeen. They deny that there is only one name under heaven whereby we can be saved.

2. Man is saved by his own works through mastering education, empowerment and enlightenment, through meditative practices such as those taught by Teresa of Avila, St. John of the Cross, and St. Ignatius Loyola, just to name a few. Although Roman Catholic by source, they have spread into almost all of Christianity in the form of teachings known as Spiritual Formation and Contemplative (Mystical) Prayer just to name a few. Though renamed with Christian names, these are the same practices used by the mystics, magicians, and astrologers for centuries in their worship of Pagan gods and thus Lucifer. Catholicism also has its followers doing the sacrament of penance to gain forgiveness of sins for themselves or others and to thus be elevated into the body of Christ.

3. As the mind becomes enlightened through the silence learned in these practices, those led of Satan, believing it to be God, come to believe that they are being elevated into a state of oneness with the divine in the quiet, thus, and becoming one with God. They are led to believe that God is in everyone and they can become gods. Further they are led by the unholy spirit's presence in the quiet, not by the Bible or Spirit of Prophecy, to determine right and wrong. They believe they can in this spirit divine (use divination to determine) what is good and evil.

See how again the three original lies (unclean spirits) are being taught this time by the beast power. There is an uncanny similarity to the dragon. In fact, its roots are deep in the mysticism of paganism which is headed up by Satan himself. Again, notice the same three lies that were presented to Eve in the garden.

1 There is no true Son of God. Therefore, there is no need for the Father/Son Spirit of God. Man will surely not die because the soul is immortal.

2 Through his own strength, enlightenment can be obtained.

3 Empowered through enlightenment, he will become like God knowing both good and evil and enter a higher state of existence.

Finally, we will now look at the third and final great apostate world religion that is identified as having these three unclean spirits being taught as doctrine. It is called the false prophet and can be identified as non-other than the Islam faith. Lest anyone should feel that this is an attack on anyone or any faith specifically, let me assure you there is nothing further from the truth. We are shown in Revelation how all religions, with the exception of the remnant, would be fallen, and that God's people would be called out of them in the power of the third angel's message of Revelation 14.

The religion of Islam is based on the teachings of a man named Muhammad, who professed to be prophet of a god named Allah. Muhammad was born Mohammad Mustafa in AD 570 and died in AD 632. At age 25, he married a 40 year old wealthy woman named Khadija, who came from a Roman Catholic convent and was basically a former nun. Her cousin, Waraquah, was also a Roman Catholic Meccan, so there was a heavy Papal influence in Muhammad's life, as can be seen in the teachings of the Koran.

Prior to his marriage, he was also heavily influenced by the pagan beliefs present in Mecca during his youth. In the Kabah, the pagan temple in Mecca, there was 360 gods that prior to Islam were worshiped. Different Arab tribes would tend to prefer different gods. History proves irrefutably that, before the Islamic religion came into existence, the Sabbeans in Arabia worshipped the moon-god Allah, who was married to the sun-goddess.

Together they had three daughters. It was also common practice to use the name of the moon-god in the Quraish tribe to which Muhammad was member in good standing.

Influenced by his wife and her cousin, Muhammad began a new hybrid religion based on Catholicism and Pagan worship of the moon god Allah. Though this is heavily debated by most of the Islamic faith (especially when attempting to convert Christians to Islam), the evidence is overwhelming.

After his wife's death in AD 622, he moved to Medina. In AD 630 he marched into Mecca. Bent on preserving some of his father's traditions, Muhammad determined to "reform" his native pagan religion. Instead of trying to completely change his Meccan brothers to a different religion, Muhammad took the top pagan god of his tribe (Allah) and chose it to be his new monotheistic god. Allah was already considered one of the top gods among the other pagan gods represented by the idols at the Kabah. Muhammad simply banished the other 359 pagan gods leaving what Muslims refer to today as "Allah". Thus Islam was born. Muhammad died two years later.

The Koran was subsequently compiled from Muhammad's writings in AD 650. These writings, and thus the Koran, were supposedly directly dictated by Mohammed from Allah. Consequently Mohammad was considered a prophet who, it is taught, gave the very words of Allah to his people. As I stated before, most of

Islam denies the pagan ties to their religion. They insist that Allah is the same as Yahweh. Let's examine this closer.

The following is quoted from the website, http://www.nccg.org /islam/Islam01-Allah.html: **"The God of the Old Testament is known as YHWH (יהוה) or, when pointed with the correct vowels, Yahweh. This translates as "The Self-Existent One", being derived from the Hebrew háwáh, meaning "to exist". As <u>Allah</u> is the name of God on the Muslim Holy Scriptures, the Koran (or Quran), so Yahweh is the Name of God in the Hebrew Scriptures, the Bible. What is particularly interesting and significant is the fact that Yahweh *never* appears as the name of *any* deity outside the Bible. There is no record anywhere of any other tribe or religion which worshipped Yahweh. The Hebrew Name of God is unique to the Bible and its chosen people. From this alone we may deduce that the Name "Yahweh" was not borrowed from some other culture or religion. It emerged uniquely within the Bible revelation.**

It is claimed by Muslims that Allah is the God of the Bible and that he is mentioned in the sacred texts. This is absolutely not true. The name "Allah" does not appear once in either the Old or New Testaments. The only time God is referred to by name in the Old Testament is either as YAHWEH (meaning "He (who) is") or as a contraction, YAH. [Please note that the name "Jehovah" is *not* a biblical name of God but was especially 'created' by Jews afraid to pronounce the Sacred Name by combining the consonants YHWH with the vowels from *adonai*, meaning "Lord"].

The word alah *does* exist in Hebrew but it is not a proper name and it *never* refers to God. It has three principal meanings: (a) to curse, swear, or adjure; (b) to lament (weep); and (c) to arise, ascend, climb, go away, leap, etc. It is an indisputable fact that ALLAH does not appear even once as the Name of God, or even of a man, in the Hebrew Scriptures. There is no word 'alah' or 'allah' in the Greek New Testament at all. It was, quite simply, unknown in the Bible world. To therefore claim that 'Allah' was the name of God in the Bible is without one single shred of evidence. God has *always* been known as Yahweh or (much less frequently) by the contraction Yah.

Muslim scholars have gone to great lengths to try and prove that the Arabic "Allah" is, in fact, the same as the Hebrew "Eloah", which is not a proper name and simply translates as "God". The words "El" and "Elohim" also translate the same way, appear far more numerously than Eloah, and may be used to designate either the true God, pagan deities, idols, or even human judges. It is for this reason that I have heard Muslim apologists get annoyed when other Muslims talk about "God" instead of "Allah" because the word "God" can be applied to any religion's god. They recognize that Allah is a proper name which distinguishes the God of the Muslims from the God of the Jews and Christians, or the gods of the Hindus and others. "Eloah" is, in any case, a derivative of "El" and its plural "Elohim" which doesn't remotely sound like "Allah". You will not find many (if any) Muslims insisting that they worship the Hebrew Eloah - the only time they ever try to make a connection is when trying to recruit Jews and Christians to Islam. If I were to confess that "Eloah" were my God and that Mohammed was his prophet I doubt any Muslim would believe I had converted to Islam!

There is another El-derived word for "God" in the Old Testament which sounds similar to Allah and that is Elah. It is only used by the prophets Ezra, Daniel and once by Jeremiah. It is, again, not a proper name, and actually also means an "oak tree" and was thus also used by pagans as a title for their tree deities, i.e. idols. I doubt somehow that Muslims would wish their Allah to be associated with an idol.

Even if the Muslim scholars were right about "Eloah" (which the evidence strongly repudiates) we would then be faced with the problem that God has two proper names - Yahweh and Eloah/Allah - which contradicts God's own testimony in the Old Testament that He is *only* known as Yahweh."

Beyond the historical and linguistic evidence, there is also much archeological evidence that Allah was the moon god to the pre-Islamic people. The above website has several pages of information showing that the moon god had many temples throughout the Middle East from the mountains of Turkey to the banks of the Nile. Archeologists show that it was the most widespread religion of that part of the ancient world.

Another evidence of its pagan origins is the symbol of Islam itself as seen in the sickle moon and star. Its roots can be traced all the way back to ancient Mesopotamia where the star/sun in the sickle moon was seen as representing the birth of the sun. The specific Mesopotamian deities were named Ashtoreth and Tammuz in that culture. Ashtoreth worship was tied to Baal or Baalim worship in the Scriptures and was one of Ahab's abhorrent sins under the evil influence of Jezebel.

"**Under the blighting influence of Ahab's rule, Israel wandered far from the living God and corrupted their ways before Him. For many years they had been losing their sense of reverence and godly fear; and now it seemed as if there were none who dared expose their lives by openly standing forth in opposition to the prevailing blasphemy. The dark shadow of apostasy covered the whole land. Images of Baalim and Ashtoreth were everywhere to be seen.**" PK page 115

In ancient Egypt this symbol was seen again in the worship of Isis and Osiris. The Sun/Moon symbol was seen on the head of Taurus the bull in Egyptian art. To the people of Egypt, the sun represented the sun god. But, it really pointed to the star of Sirius to the priests of that religion. Sirius is known among most esoteric occultist circles as the star of Lucifer or the all seeing eye of Lucifer.

In Assyria and Babylon the sickle/sun deity was Baal-Hadad, which is the same as the Baal or Bel worship condemned in the Old Testament. These symbols of the Crescent Moon and Sun/Star in all these religions always represented the general male and female regenerative powers of nature according to the "Encyclopedia of Free Masonry". It is actually a form of nature worship or pantheism. Many sexual perversions and orgy practices were associated with both Baal and Ashtoreth worship.

According to Robert A. Morey in his book "Islam Unveiled", on pg. 46, he shows that the Encyclopedia of Religion mentions that Allah is a pre-Islamic name ... corresponding to the Babylonian Bel. He also points out in this book that Allah was the moon god who married the sun goddess. Together they produced 3 goddesses who were called the Daughters of Allah. Their names were Al-Lat, Al-Uzza, and Manat.

What is unique is how Catholicism uses the same symbols in the mass where the disk sun shaped wafer is placed in the symbol of the sickle shaped moon prior to being given to the believer as a symbol of Christ's body. Both religions also teach the doctrine of the holy, virgin mother Mary. It should be clear by now that Islam is a unique religion being a hybrid of pagan moon god worship and Catholicism. Although many, if not most, of its believers claim to be unaware of this, it is none the less true.

What is important to this book and to the reader are the teachings of this religion in light of the Biblical truth. First and foremost is the teaching that Jesus is not the Son of God but just a messenger or prophet of God. Islam teaches that all prophets are equal, so Jesus is demoted to the level of all other prophets. Another way to look at it is that Muhammad promoted himself to the level of Jesus. The Koran mentions Jesus 25 times and states that Jesus was born to Mary by virginal conception. It denies that He was killed or crucified and teaches that He ascended to heaven without seeing death.

Some Islamic sects look for Jesus to return from the earth (not in the clouds of heaven with great glory) with Al-Mahdī who was born in AD 869. He is believed to be the twelfth Imam or great prophet. It is taught that he escaped death in a well and will return in the name of Mohammed and Allah. Through sharia law, he will fill the earth (seen now as filled with injustice and tyranny) with peace and justice.

If Allah was the same god as the Hebrew God then for Muhammad to prophesy that Jesus did not die for our sins makes him a false prophet. The Bible states that Christ is the Lamb of God slain from the foundation of the world. All credible evidence denies that Allah is the same god as the Yahweh. Either way, during no time in the history of the world has any singular false prophet or pagan god had a following as large as Muhammad and

Allah. Indeed Islamic followers now are numbering in the billions.

In light of this and the political power and terrorism exercised against the world in the name of Allah, let's read the quote again made over a hundred years ago by God's prophet. "**As we near the close of time, there will be greater and still greater external parade of heathen power; heathen deities will manifest their signal power, and will exhibit themselves before the cities of the world; and this delineation has already begun to be fulfilled. By a variety of images the Lord Jesus represented to John the wicked character and seductive influence of those who have been distinguished for their persecution of God's people. All need wisdom carefully to search out the mystery of iniquity that figures so largely in the winding up of this earth's history. . . ."** EV 705 The events that took place on 9/11/2001 in New York are just a beginning of what is to come. The ultimate goal of Islam is to advance Allah's will to the entire world even by Jihad (violence and force) when necessary.

In the teachings of the Koran is the concept that we can come directly to Allah without Jesus. Islam teaches the sustained existence of the soul and a transformed physical existence after death. Muslims accept that there will be a day of judgment when all individuals will be divided between the eternal destinations of paradise and hell.

A Muslim author on IslamOnline.net explains the nature of hell in this way: **"Ultimately, God will remove from Hell those believers whose sins were not forgiven nor atoned for by good deeds in their lifetimes, and they will then enter Paradise. The remaining inhabitants of Hell will stay there eternally."** If you are an unbeliever, you will burn in hell forever. Sound familiar? There even seems to be a type of purgatory.

For those who do go to paradise, the Koran's teachings are interpreted in different ways. Wikipedia describes it in the following way. **"The Islamic texts describes life for its immortal inhabitants as: one that is happy — without hurt, sorrow, fear or shame — where every wish is fulfilled. Traditions relate that inhabitants will be of the same age (33 years), and of the same standing/equal. Their life is one of bliss including: wearing costly robes, bracelets, perfumes as they partake in exquisite banquets, served in priceless vessels by immortal youths, as they recline on couches inlaid with gold or precious stones. Other foods mentioned include meats, scented wine and clear drinks bringing neither drunkenness nor rousing quarrelling."**

This is the most benign of the descriptions. There are others that involve the debasement of women and describe the use of ninety-nine virgins by those favored by Allah as sexual slaves to the saved elite. In these descriptions of Jannah, the existence for women is a nightmare. In some sects of Islam, the more violent you are against other religious systems of belief (the Jihad to enforce Allah's will upon the world), the more rewarded (with virgins and wealth) you will be in the afterlife.

Although a symbolic tie at most, it is interesting, in light of Allah's pagan roots in Egyptian worship of Osiris and the all seeing eye of Lucifer in the star of Sirius, that in their Heaven (Jannah) all are age 33. This is the same number as the enlightened level in the Scottish Rite of Free Masonry where it becomes fully known that they worship the all seeing eye of Lucifer.

Now let's review Revelation 16:13 again. *"And I saw three unclean spirits like frogs come out of the mouth of the dragon, and out of the mouth of the beast, and out of the mouth of the false prophet. "* We will now view these three unclean spirits, as seen in the doctrines of Islam.

1. They deny that Christ is the true Son of God. They see Him as a messenger of Allah and deny His death on the cross and resurrection for the sinner. Man is also presented as having an immortal soul and thus cannot (or surely will not) die. They deny the Father/Son relationship essentiality in their salvation as seen in the prayer of John chapter seventeen.

2. They are saved by your own works. Through pilgrimages to Mecca and other good works one becomes more enlightened by the prophets and can work to shorten time in hell or even earn

Jannah (Heaven). The ultimate goal is to advance Allah's will to the entire world even by Jihad (violence and force) when necessary.

3   Once in paradise one may have all his wishes and thus have an elevated state of godlike bliss. To quote Jim Mitchell in his book Islam (The Final Chapter) in regard to heaven: **"A Muslim thinks in terms of the comforts of a refreshing oasis, circled with ready to harvest date trees, and populated with young olive eyed virgins ready for the taking."**

See how the three original lies (unclean spirits) are again being taught this time by Islam. There is an uncanny similarity to Catholicism and paganism. In fact, its roots are deep in both. Again notice the same three lies that were presented to Eve in the garden.

1   There is no true Son of God. Therefore, there is no need the Father/Son Spirit of God and man will surely not die because his soul is immortal.

2   Through his own strength he can obtain enlightenment.

3 Empowered through enlightenment he will become like or at one with God knowing both good and evil and enter a higher state of existence.

Now that we have seen the three major systems of religion that would teach the three doctrines (unclean spirits), we will now see how the cross is both attacked by, and is an answer to, these doctrines as seen in the sanctuary.

Chapter 9
Revelations of the Cross In the Sanctuary
Part 1 - The North

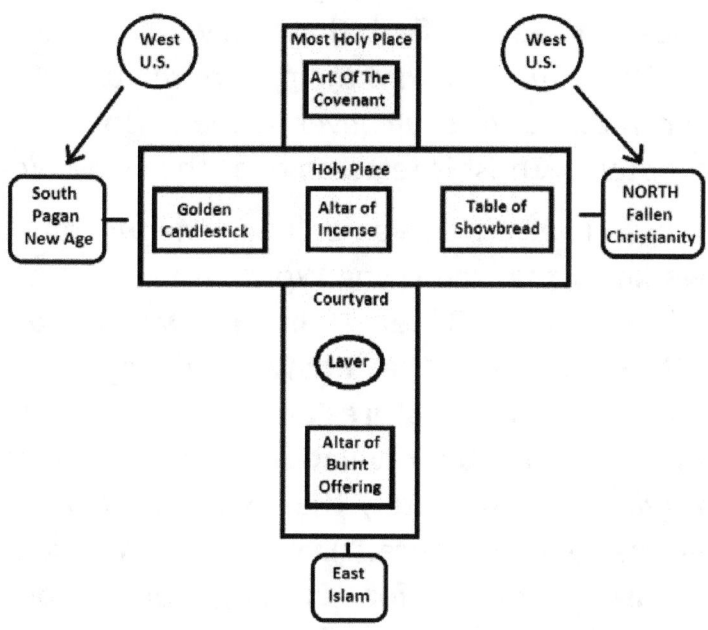

Here you see a diagram of the cross as it lays over the design of the sanctuary and its furniture in each of the different compartments. You will notice that each piece of furniture has a representation of a specific truth concerning Christ's death on the cross. This truth will match in a unique way to the attacks or false doctrines that are brought by the corresponding religious system.

It was no coincidence that God had the furniture laid out the way it was.

We will begin with the table of showbread that was on the side of the north. In Daniel 11, the King of the North is a description of Fallen Christianity with Papal Rome (mother of harlots) as the leader. So let's look at what the table of showbread represents. In John 6:51, Jesus said: *"I am the living bread"*. Later, He taught that unless you eat His flesh that you would have no life in you. *"And Jesus said unto them, I am the bread of life: he that cometh to me shall never hunger;"* (John 6:35). In John chapter 1, Christ is referred to as the living Word.

Christ is also revealed to us in the written word. Thus we know that the Living Word also correlates with the written word (Bible). **"In His word, God has committed to men the knowledge necessary for salvation. The Holy Scriptures are to be accepted as an authoritative, infallible revelation of His will. They are the standard of character, the revealer of doctrines, and the test of experience. "Every scripture inspired of God is also profitable for teaching, for reproof, for correction, for instruction which is in righteousness; that the man of God may be complete, furnished completely unto every good work." 2 Timothy 3:16, 17, R.V."** GC vii.1

"Satan well knew that the Holy Scriptures would enable men to discern his deceptions and withstand his power. It was by the word that even the Saviour of the world had resisted his attacks. At every assault, Christ

presented the shield of eternal truth, saying, "It is written." To every suggestion of the adversary, he opposed the wisdom and power of the word. In order for Satan to maintain his sway over men, and establish the authority of the Papal usurper, he must keep them in ignorance of the Scriptures. The Bible would exalt God, and place finite men in their true position; therefore its sacred truths must be concealed and suppressed. This logic was adopted by the Roman Church. For hundreds of years the circulation of the Bible was prohibited." GC 51

What doctrines of Roman Catholicism would attack the truths of the table of showbread? First, there is the attack on the word of God in both of its forms. It has attacked the Bible through suppressing it and also by changing God's unchangeable times and laws as seen in Daniel 7. *"And he shall speak great words against the most High, and shall wear out the saints of the most High, and think to change times and laws:"* (Daniel 7:25) We have seen how Rome has changed God's Ten Commandments to allow idolatry and has changed God's holy Sabbath day to Sunday.

Secondly, Rome and fallen Christianity have attacked the real Word (Christ) in His relationship to His Father through the trinity doctrine in all its various forms. As we will see further on in this book, without this error revealed and the truth about God in it proper place, it is impossible for God's people to be sanctified.

Also in the mass, the Papacy teaches that the bread becomes the literal crucified flesh of Christ thus killing Jesus over and over again. Paul tells us *"Knowing that Christ being raised from the dead dieth no more; death hath no more dominion over him. For in that he died, he died unto sin once: but in that he liveth, he liveth unto God."* (Romans 6:10-11) Here we see that Christ need only die once for the sins of the word, not over and over again as seen in the celebration of mass.

In the second false doctrine from this religious system, we saw an attack in the form of spiritualism. It is carried out through the education of mystical teachings that train individuals in the practice of contemplative prayer and spiritual formation. These have their roots tied to the teachings of Roman Catholic mystics such as Teresa of Avila, St John of the Cross, and St. Ignatius Loyola (founder of the Jesuit order).

In these practices, the real Spirit of Jesus in the heart is replaced by Satan's demonic counterparts who fool those who practice these mystical rites into believing they are in the presence of God. Thus they become "enlightened". Teresa of Avila was said to have even levitated during these mystical trances. Yet, the Bible teaches: *"Draw nigh to God, and he will draw nigh to you. Cleanse your hands, ye sinners; and purify your hearts, ye double minded. Be afflicted, and mourn, and weep: let your laughter be turned to mourning, and your joy to heaviness. Humble yourselves in the sight of the Lord, and he shall lift you up."* (James 4:8-10) It is through afflicting our souls before God and through heartfelt repentance and renouncing of sin that He lifts us up, not by mystical meditation.

The third attack lies in the promise that through these practices we will attain a state of higher existence through this enlightenment and be like God. It attacks the truth that it is in Christ that we through adoption become sons of God through the grace of Jesus and the love of the Father. *"Not of works, lest any man should boast."* (Ephesians 2:9)

Therefore, the defense of the remnant church is to hold to the truths of Christ by faith, as seen in the table of showbread, and thus not fall to these attacks. These corrupt teachings will be evident in all of fallen Christianity. It is through the truth of the cross, as seen in the table of showbread, that we are to reach out to fallen Christianity calling God's people out of Babylon.

"As the teachings of Spiritualism are accepted by the churches, the restraint imposed upon the carnal heart is removed, and the profession of religion will become a cloak to conceal the basest iniquity. A belief in spiritual manifestations opens the door to seducing spirits, and doctrines of devils, and thus the influence of evil angels will be felt in the churches.

Of Babylon, at the time brought to view in this prophecy, it is declared, *"Her sins have reached unto heaven, and God hath remembered her iniquities."* **[Revelation 18:5.] She has filled up the measure of her**

guilt, and destruction is about to fall upon her. But God still has a people in Babylon; and before the visitation of his judgments, these faithful ones must be called out, that they *"partake not of her sins, and receive not of her plagues.""* GC88 603

It is in an appropriate response to the first part of the attack by fallen Christianity that we share the three angel's messages in the love of the cross. Remember that the first part of the beast's attack is on the word (Bible) and the Word (Christ). The attack on the Scriptures is especially seen in the attack on the character of God as expressed in His Ten Commandments.

Chief among these attacks is the onslaught against the first, second, and fourth commandments. Therefore, the call out of Babylon should be in the light of presenting the true gospel of Christ and His redeeming love in the light of these three commandments. It is in the illumination of the three following facts that we reveal this attack on God's law of love. The cross of Christ shines on the commandments of God.

1. Revealing the true nature of God as seen in His Son and thus His People.
2. Showing how man has become his own idol to replace God.
3. Revealing the true Sabbath rest as found in dying to self and taking on the yoke of Christ.

Only in acknowledging the truth that Jesus died for our complete redemption can we truly see the Father's nature exemplified, allow our nature (idolatry of self) to die with Christ, and then rest in the knowledge and power of His redeeming grace. Then, we can fully understand the power and joy of resting in God. There we learn that in keeping God's sanctified Sabbath we acknowledge Him as our Creator both originally and again in the recreation of our fallen nature into His sinless divine nature.

Remember that John chapter one reveals that Jesus, who is the actual son of God, is also the Creator who sanctified the Sabbath. Attacks that undermine the Creator or His holy Sabbath day will effectively prevent the true gift of the Sabbath rest (sanctification) in the Christian life.

"God denounces Babylon "because she made all nations drink of the wine of the wrath of her fornication.". . . God made the world in six days and rested on the seventh, sanctifying this day, and setting it apart from all others as holy to Himself, to be observed by His people throughout their generations. But the man of sin, exalting himself above God, sitting in the temple of God, and showing himself to be God, thought to change times and laws. This power, thinking to prove that it was not only equal to God, but above God, changed the rest day, placing the first day of the week where the seventh should be. And the Protestant world has taken this child of the papacy to be regarded

as sacred. In the word of God this is called her fornication. [Revelation 14:8]

During the Christian dispensation the great enemy of man's happiness has made the Sabbath of the fourth commandment an object of special attack. Satan says, "I will work at cross purposes with God. I will <u>empower</u> my followers to set aside God's memorial, the seventh-day Sabbath. Thus I will show the world that the day sanctified and blessed by God has been changed. That day shall not live in the minds of the people. I will obliterate the memory of it. I will place in its stead a day that does not bear the credentials of God, a day that cannot be a sign between God and His people. I will lead those who accept this day to place upon it the sanctity that God placed upon the seventh day."--<u>PK</u> 183, 184 (c. 1914)." (<u>LDE</u> 123.3)

"The world is given to idolatry, and they have forgotten God, their Maker and Preserver. They openly transgress his law, trample on the Sabbath, and in thus doing break the fourth commandment of the decalogue. Instead of keeping God's own rest-day, which he sanctified after he had rested upon it, and set it apart for man to observe and reverence, they honor a Papal institution" (<u>RH</u> Sept 16, 1862)

In Satan's second lie, Papal Rome and apostate Protestantism have also attacked the cross through its teachings of mysticism and spiritualism within the church. Note that the table of showbread was on the north side. Satan speaking of himself said "... **I will** ascend into heaven, I will exalt my throne above the stars of God: I will sit also upon the mount of the congregation, in the sides of the north: I will ascend above the heights of the clouds; I will be like the most High." (Isaiah 14:13-14)

In the teachings as taught by Teresa of Avila, St. John of the Cross, and St. Ignatius Loyola, the doctrines of ancient mysticism that are rooted deeply in Satanism are being subtly introduced into the all churches; and yes, even into the remnant church. It has brought the concepts of spiritual formation and contemplative prayer (in the silence) into our very midst. In these doctrines, those deceived will be led from Christ, the living Word, to inadvertently worshiping Satan. In this they will feel power and receive new "light" and believe it to be revelations of God. But this attack that is in the holy place of the tabernacle is brought through not understanding the truth of Christ as demonstrated in the table of showbread.

"Then I saw the Father rise from the throne and in a flaming chariot go into the Holy of Holies within the vail, and did sit. There I saw thrones which I had not seen before. Then Jesus rose up from the throne, and most of those who were bowed down rose up with him ... Angels were all about the chariot as it came where Jesus was; he stepped into it and was borne to the Holiest where the Father sat. Then I beheld Jesus as he was before the Father a great High Priest ... Then I turned to look at the company who were still bowed

before the throne. They did not know that Jesus had left it. Satan appeared to be by the throne trying to carry on the work of God. I saw them look up to the throne and pray, My Father give us thy spirit. Then Satan would breathe on them an unholy influence. In it there was light and much power, but no sweet love, joy and peace. Satan's object was to keep them deceived and to draw back and deceive God's children. (DS, March 14, 1846)

Those who are not rooted in the sanctuary truth, and still see Jesus' grace of the cross as being ministered from the holy place, will fall to Satan's overwhelming delusions. Yes, there will be power and light but not from God. If we eat the bread of life as represented as the unleavened bread on the table of showbread, we acknowledge our dependence on Christ as our High Priest. We will follow him, as seen in the doctrine of the sanctuary, into the holy of holies and thus not fall to this counterfeit christ.

It should be noted that saying we believe that Christ has gone into the most holy place and actually going there with Him is two very different things. It is in the most holy place that Christ and the Father (through their Spirit) actually sanctify those who follow Jesus there. If we don't understand who it is that is sanctifying us or if we refuse to allow this sanctifying work in our lives, we are not following Christ into that most holy union with the Father. Only then can we truly understand the truth revealed and realized in the Day of

Atonement. If left in the holy place, the sanctifying power of the cross cannot and will not be realized by God's remnant church.

Yet, in the third part of the beasts attack is the promise of reaching that higher state of existence without Christ. Thomas Merton, one of the teachers and proponents of contemplative prayer, in his book "The New Man" sums it up this way. **"Contemplation is a mark of a fully mature Christian life. It makes the believer no longer a slave or a servant of a Divine Master, no longer the fearful keeper of a difficult law, no longer even an obedient and submissive son who is still too young to participate in his Father's counsels. Contemplation is that wisdom which makes man the friend of God, a thing which Aristotle thought to be impossible. For how, he said, can a man be God's friend? Friendship implies equality. That is precisely the message of the Gospel."** Pg. 17

Note that in this teaching we are no longer a servant of God. No longer are we even obedient sons of God. We are alleged to be equal with Jesus and able to enter into the Father's Counsels. Remember that Ellen White showed us that Jesus was the only being in the universe that could enter into the counsels of the Father because He was equal with His Father. Thus in this teaching we see that we become as Gods.

1. There is no true Son of God. Therefore, there is no need the Father/Son Spirit of God and man will surely not die because his soul is immortal.

2 Through his own strength, enlightenment can be obtained.

3 Empowered through enlightenment, man will become like or at one with God knowing both good and evil and enter a higher state of existence.

Pope John Paul II confirmed this at the opening of the new millennium. **"The great mystical tradition of the Church of both East and West ... shows how prayer can progress, as a genuine dialogue of love, to the point of rendering the person wholly possessed by the divine Beloved, vibrating at the Spirit's touch, resting filially within the Father's heart. This is the lived experience of Christ's promise: "He who loves me will be loved by my Father, and I will love him and manifest myself to him" (John 14:21). It is a journey totally sustained by grace, which nonetheless demands an intense spiritual commitment and is no stranger to painful purifications (the "dark night"). But it leads, in various possible ways, to the ineffable joy experienced by the mystics as "nuptial union". How can we forget here, among the many shining examples, the teachings of St John of the Cross and saint Teresa of Avila?"** The Pope even states that it is through the doctrines of this mystical prayer and formative spirituality, as seen in these Catholic mystics, that Catholicism will evangelize the world. It is not through spiritualism that we, the true church, will evangelize the world but through the good news of the Gospel of Jesus Christ and Him crucified.

Remember that only the priests were to eat of the showbread. Thus only through Jesus as our high priest in heaven can we enter the holy of holies and be perfected in the life of Christ. **"The showbread was kept ever before the Lord as a perpetual offering. . . . It was called showbread, or "bread of the presence," because it was ever before the face of the Lord. It was an acknowledgment of man's dependence upon God for both temporal and spiritual food, and that it is received only through the mediation of Christ"** (FLB 197)

Hence, we see that the unclean demonic doctrines of the beast are answered in the truth of the cross as seen in the sanctuary and the table of showbread. It is the truth obtained from the unaltered word of God (Bible) that leads us to the Living Word (Christ). The Father brings Christ into us who sanctifies us into oneness with the Father. With their indwelling Spirit we are then able and compelled to reach out to a fallen world.

As you see this truth and begin to share and defend it among your fellow believers, do not be surprised if some of you get stiff resistance to this truth. The hypnotic and beguiling nature of these false doctrines has its talons deep within many believers and they will not give it up easily. *"Now the Spirit speaketh expressly, that in the latter times some shall depart from the faith, giving heed to seducing spirits, and doctrines of devils."* (1st Timothy 4:1) Only in giving heed to the testimonies of God can we be freed through God's redeeming power.

Satan designed his three lies to prevent you from receiving the gift of God's Spirit in its true nature. By now we should be beginning to see that the promises of what Satan offers through his lies are but the shadows or perversions of what God has in store for those who follow Him. Now let's turn our eyes to the south.

Revelations of the Cross In the Sanctuary
Part 2 - The South

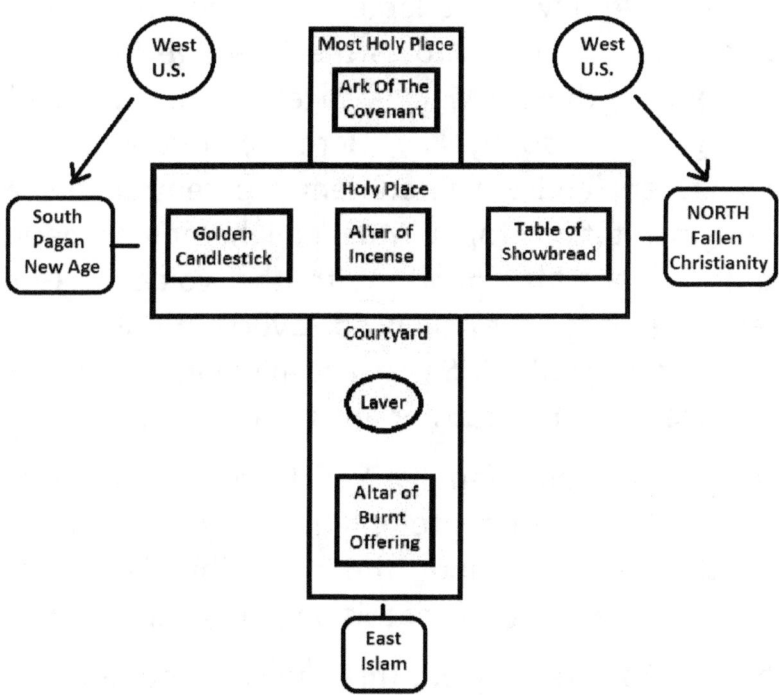

Again we see a diagram of the cross as it lays over the design of the sanctuary and its furniture in each of the different compartments. Again I would like you to notice that each piece of furniture has a representation of a specific truth concerning the cross of Christ. This truth will match in a unique way to the attack that is brought by the corresponding religious system.

We will look at the golden lamp stand that was on the side of the south in the holy place. As we learned earlier, this system is referred to as the dragon power who had been identified as Lucifer. We also learned that it was represented by the pagan and eastern religions of the world. We now see a large movement in the world today generally referred to as the New Age Movement that is pulling these religions together into a singular new age philosophy. Here meditation, self-empowerment and enlightenment are central themes. In these meditations for spiritual enlightenment, people learn to silence the mind. With the voice of God's protection (conscience) silenced, over time and in the form of "spirit guides", Satan and his angels take over the mind leading men farther and farther from God.

Does this sound familiar? It is the same as the spiritual formation or contemplative prayer teachings of fallen Christianity without the new Christian names. Let's review the doctrines of this pagan system again.

In this apostate religion, three unclean doctrines are seen coming from its mouth (teachings). Their teachings are:

1. They deny that Christ is the Son of God. They either deny His existence totally or they see Him as an individual who became enlightened and was elevated into the oneness with the divine. He thus becomes equal to Buddha and other great gurus in joining the great cosmic energy matrix pattern that forms God. In this

state some refer to him now as the cosmic Christ. The soul is immortal and thus will not surely die. They either pass on into the God–Energy-Matrix or they are reincarnated.

2 They are saved by their own works through mastering education, empowerment and enlightenment through meditative practices such as mantras, and meditating on a flame to silence the mind. This is commonly known as Spiritual Formation or Contemplative/Mystical Prayer. Reliance on self (god or goddess of reason).

3 As the mind becomes enlightened, they experience Kundalini where energy coiled at the base of the spine like a serpent is released and travels up through the chakra energy centers in the body elevating them into a state of oneness with the divine in the quiet. There they are led by spirit guides (often supposed dead loved ones or past life friends) thus becoming one with the God–Energy-Matrix. In this oneness they can experience past life experiences and astral projection. It is known by such that God exists in every living thing thus they can become gods. Pantheism, in short, is alive and doing very well.

Again, notice that under this set of doctrines or beliefs that there is no such thing as sin, and you have no need of a Savior. Therefore, Jesus is not God's Son slain from the foundation of the world. Also, everyone through effective meditation into the silence and effective use of reason can be as gods. Notice that the same three part lie given to our first parents still exists.

1. There is no true Son of God. Therefore there is no for need the Father/Son Spirit of God and man will surely not die because his soul is immortal.
2. Through his own strength he can obtain enlightenment.
3. Empowered through enlightenment he will become like or at one with God knowing both good and evil and enter a higher state of existence.

Now let's review these doctrines in light of the golden lamp stand. Notice again that the lamp stand is in the holy place of the sanctuary on the south side. In the Scriptures, Egypt is often used as a symbol of sin and idolatry. Not only is it literally south of Israel but was the nation that enslaved Israel and introduced idolatry and sun worship into Israel's society. We have already seen how much of idolatry has its roots in ancient Egypt. It is also well documented that one of the first trinity doctrines was seen in Egypt in the worship of Isis, Osiris, and Horus.

The symbology as seen in the sanctuary in defending the truths of the cross are in understanding what God was showing us in the golden lamp stand. We will again examine these truths in light of the three unclean spirits or lies of the fallen systems.

The first lie if you remember was that you can deny the Son/Father relationship of God and you surely will not die. The first truth of the lamp stand we will look at, in response to this lie, lies in the very fact that it provides light. Paul said *"For God, who commanded the light to shine out of darkness, hath shined in our hearts, to give the light of the knowledge of the glory of God in the face of Jesus Christ".* (2Corinthians 4:6) Jesus said, "I am the way, the truth, and the life: no man cometh unto the Father, but by me." (John 14:6) This truth shows that our high priest, Jesus, is the conduit of the true source of light and that no man can come unto the Father except through Him. Thus the true source of light is seen in the Father and Son.

Let's remember how earlier we read where Ellen White was shown that at the beginning of the investigative judgment that the Father went into the most holy place and then Jesus followed Him. Jesus further stated, *"I am the light of the world: he that followeth me shall not walk in darkness, but shall have the light of life."* (John 8:12) Jesus was showing us, God's remnant church, that we must follow Him (the light of truth) into the most holy place of the sanctuary.

We further see, in the text above, that life cometh only in following Christ's light. In these truths, the first lie of Satan is illuminated as the deception it is. **"Christ has made every provision that His church shall be a** transformed body, illumined with the Light of the world, possessing the glory of Emmanuel. It is His purpose that every Christian shall be surrounded with a spiritual atmosphere of light and peace. He desires that we shall reveal His own joy in our lives." COL 420

In Satan's second lie to our parents, he told them that they could by their own efforts become enlightened. Yet the great prophet Isaiah in chapter eight, verse twenty stated: *"To the law and to the testimony: if they speak not according to this word, it is because there is no light in them."* The law is God's Ten Commandments and shows us that we should have no other gods than Him. Further the law shows us in the fourth commandment that our worship is rightly Christ's because He is our Creator.

Our light comes only when we have Jesus and His Father completely in our hearts and living in our lives. Satan knows this and thus directs his anger against those who reveal the truth concerning his second great lie. *"And the dragon was wroth with the woman* (God's remnant church), *and went to make war with the remnant of her seed, which keep the commandments of God, and have the testimony of Jesus Christ."* The cross of Christ as seen in the lamp stand shows that Christ is the only source of true enlightenment.

In many of the pagan (dragon) religions, the sun and moon are often seen as gods that could bring enlightenment. But, the Bible teaches differently. *"The sun shall be no more thy light by day; neither for brightness shall the moon give light unto thee: but the LORD shall be unto thee an everlasting light, and thy God thy glory."*(Isaiah 60:19) We, therefore, see that there is no enlightenment outside of the cross of Christ lived in the life of the believer.

The third lie of the dragon is that through this new age philosophy we can become as gods knowing both good and evil. What makes this interesting is that the lie is two-fold in nature. The Hebrew word for "knowing" is the word "ידע " pronounced yaw-dah and is the same word used where the Bible states that Adam k*new* (yaw-dah) Eve. Satan's claim suggests that God has an intimacy with both good and evil. This lie was intimating, to Eve then and to the New Age believer now, a duality of good and evil in God's very nature. We see this still propagated in the symbol of the yin yang in eastern and new age philosophy. But there is no duality in God's nature. His character is holy and all together righteous.

The light of the lamp stand comes from the combination of the lamp and the oil burning within the lamp. Indeed, we see in the parable of the 10 virgins that those ready to go in with Christ into the marriage feast were those that had both the lamp and the oil. *"Then shall the kingdom of heaven be likened unto ten virgins, which took their lamps, and went forth to meet the bridegroom. And five of them were wise, and five were foolish. They that were foolish took their lamps, and took no oil with them: But the wise took oil in their vessels with their lamps. While the bridegroom tarried, they all slumbered and slept. And at midnight there was a cry made, Behold, the bridegroom cometh; go ye out to meet him. Then all those virgins arose, and trimmed their lamps. And the foolish said unto the wise, Give us of your oil; for our lamps are gone out. But the wise answered, saying, Not so; lest there be not enough for us and you: but go ye rather to them that sell, and buy for yourselves. And while they went to buy, the bridegroom came; and they that were ready went in with him to the marriage: and the door was shut. Afterward came also the other virgins, saying, Lord, Lord, open to us. But he answered and said, Verily I say unto you, I know you not."* (Matthew 25:1-12)

It seems that to have a lamp is not enough. One must have the oil as well. It is essential to our salvation. "**As Christ sat looking upon the party that waited for the bridegroom, He told His disciples the story of the ten virgins, by their experience illustrating the experience of the church that shall live just before His second coming. The two classes of watchers represent the two classes who profess to be waiting for their Lord. They are called virgins because they profess a pure faith. By the lamps is represented the word of God. The psalmist says, "Thy word is a lamp unto my feet, and a light unto my path." Psalm 119:105.**

The oil is a symbol of the Holy Spirit. Thus the Spirit is represented in the prophecy of Zechariah. "The angel that talked with me came again," he says, "and waked me, as a man that is wakened out of his sleep, and said

unto me, What seest thou? And I said, I have looked, and behold a candlestick all of gold, with a bowl upon the top of it, and his seven lamps thereon, and seven pipes to the seven lamps, which are upon the top thereof; and two olive trees by it, one upon the right side of the bowl, and the other upon the left side thereof. So I answered and spake to the angel that talked with me, saying, What are these, my lord? . . . Then he answered and spake unto me, saying, This is the word of the Lord unto Zerubbabel, saying, Not by might, nor by power, but by My Spirit, saith the Lord of hosts." COL 406-407

Those who find Jesus in the cross of Christ as seen in the sanctuary will have more than just knowledge of Him in the word. They will be baptized into His and His Father's Spirit. *"And when the day of Pentecost was fully come, they were all with one accord in one place. And suddenly there came a sound from heaven as of a rushing mighty wind, and it filled all the house where they were sitting. And there appeared unto them cloven tongues like as of fire, and it sat upon each of them. And they were all filled with the Holy Ghost, and began to speak with other tongues, as the Spirit gave them utterance."* (Acts 2:1-4)

"The plant grows by receiving that which God has provided to sustain its life. It sends down its roots into the earth. It drinks in the sunshine, the dew, and the rain. It receives the life-giving properties from the air. So the Christian is to grow by co-operating with the divine agencies. Feeling our helplessness, we are to improve all the opportunities granted us to gain a fuller experience. As the plant takes root in the soil, so we are to take deep root in Christ. As the plant receives the sunshine, the dew, and the rain, we are to open our hearts to the Holy Spirit. The work is to be done "not by might, nor by power, <u>but by My Spirit</u>, saith the Lord of hosts." Zechariah 4:6. If we keep our minds stayed upon Christ, He will come unto us "as the rain, as the latter and former rain unto the earth." Hosea 6:3. As the Sun of Righteousness, He will arise upon us "with healing in His wings." Malachi 4:2. We shall "grow as the lily." We shall "revive as the corn, and grow as the vine." Hosea 14:5, 7. By constantly relying upon Christ as our personal Saviour, we shall grow up into Him in all things who is our head." <u>COL</u> 66

Now we see the truth of the lamp stand in the sanctuary. It is when Christ returns with His Father in the heart of the true believer that we become God's vessel of light shining to the world. In John 14, when telling His disciples of His return as the Comforter, Christ stated: *"And I will pray the Father, and he shall give you another Comforter, that he may abide with you for ever; Even the Spirit of truth; whom the world cannot receive, because it seeth him not, neither knoweth him: but ye know him; for he dwelleth with you, and shall be in you. I will not leave you comfortless: I will come to you. At that day ye shall know that I am in my Father, and ye in me, and I in you. He that hath my commandments, and keepeth them, he it is that loveth me: and he that loveth me shall be loved of my Father, and I will love him, and will manifest myself to him. ... If a man love me, he will keep my words: and my Father will love him, and we will come unto him, and make our abode with him."* (John 14:16-18, 20-23)

"Ye are the light of the world. A city that is set on an hill cannot be hid. Neither do men light a candle, and put it under a bushel, but on a candlestick; and it giveth light unto all that are in the house. Let your light so shine before men, that they may see your good works, and glorify your Father which is in heaven." (Matthew 5:14-16)

Here is the truth and answer to Satan's third lie of becoming like gods. It is in surrendering to the Holy Spirit that we take on the divine nature of God and become a light to the world through Christ's divine nature imparted to us. There is no knowledge (Yaw-dah) of good and evil for the sanctified individual. God is pure and is only good. Christ when called good master stated *"there is none good but one, that is, God: but if thou wilt enter into life, keep the commandments."* (Matthew 19:17) The life of the true believer is changed into His image and is thus enabled to live within the boundaries of God's law.

You may ask if this is really possible. It is a fact that if we are fully baptized by the combined Spirit of the Father and Son, with our hearts fully submitted to Christ's control, that we can be totally cleansed of our fallen nature of sin. This lies at the heart of the Gospel shining forth from the cross of Christ. Among the significant virtues of the lamp stand is that it has seven lamps. The number seven stands for not only God and His perfection but also for spiritual completeness as seen in finally resting in God's true Sabbath truth. In this is seen the promise of true sanctification.

"All true obedience comes from the heart. It was heart work with Christ. And if we consent, He will so identify Himself with our thoughts and aims, so blend our hearts and minds into conformity to His will, that when obeying Him we shall be but carrying out our own impulses. The will, refined and sanctified, will find its highest delight in doing His service. When we know God as it is our privilege to know Him, our life will be a life of continual obedience. Through an appreciation of the character of Christ, through communion with God, sin will become hateful to us." DA 668

Again, we see that the promises which Satan offers through his lies are but a shadow or perversion of what God has in store for those who follow Him. I finish this section with both a promise and warning for God's remnant church.

In the parable of the ten virgins, **"The two classes of watchers represent the two classes who profess to be waiting for their Lord. They are called virgins because they profess a pure faith. By the lamps is represented the word of God. The psalmist says, "Thy word is a lamp unto my feet, and a light unto my path." The oil is** a symbol of the Holy Spirit. Thus the Spirit is represented in the prophecy of Zechariah. . . . "I have looked, and behold a candlestick all of gold, with a bowl upon the top of it, and his seven lamps thereon, and seven pipes to the seven lamps, . . . and two olive trees by it." . . . From the two olive trees the golden oil was emptied through the golden pipes into the bowl of the candlestick, and thence into the golden lamps that gave light to the sanctuary.

So from the holy ones that stand in God's presence His Spirit is imparted to the human instrumentalities who are consecrated to His service. The mission of the two anointed ones is to communicate to God's people that heavenly grace which alone can make His word a lamp to the feet and a light to the path. "Not by might, nor by power, but by my spirit, saith the Lord of hosts."

In the parable, all the ten virgins went out to meet the bridegroom. All had lamps and vessels for oil. For a time there was seen no difference between them. So with the church that lives just before Christ's second coming. All have a knowledge of the Scriptures. All have heard the message of Christ's near approach, and confidently expect His appearing. But as in the parable, so it is now. A time of waiting intervenes, faith is tried; and when the cry is heard, "Behold, the bridegroom cometh," . . . many are unready. They have no oil in their vessels with their lamps. They are destitute of the Holy Spirit. . . . The theory of truth, unaccompanied by the Holy Spirit, cannot quicken the soul or sanctify the heart.

One may be familiar with the commands and promises of the Bible; but unless the Spirit of God sets the truth home, the character will not be transformed. Without the enlightenment of the Spirit, men will not be able to distinguish truth from error, and they will fall under the masterful temptations of Satan. . . . Character is not transferable. No man can believe for another. No man can receive the Spirit for another. No man can impart to another the character which is the fruit of the Spirit's working." COL, 406-412

The knowledge of truth is not enough. If we are to be a light unto the world, we must have the Spirit of the only two who can light up the most holy place in the sanctuary. We must follow them and in the Holiest of Holies be baptized by their Spirit. Only in having a real and lasting relationship with Jesus and the Father (the only sources of oil) can we find and reflect the light of God to the dark and lost world.

Revelations of the Cross In the Sanctuary
Part 3 - The East

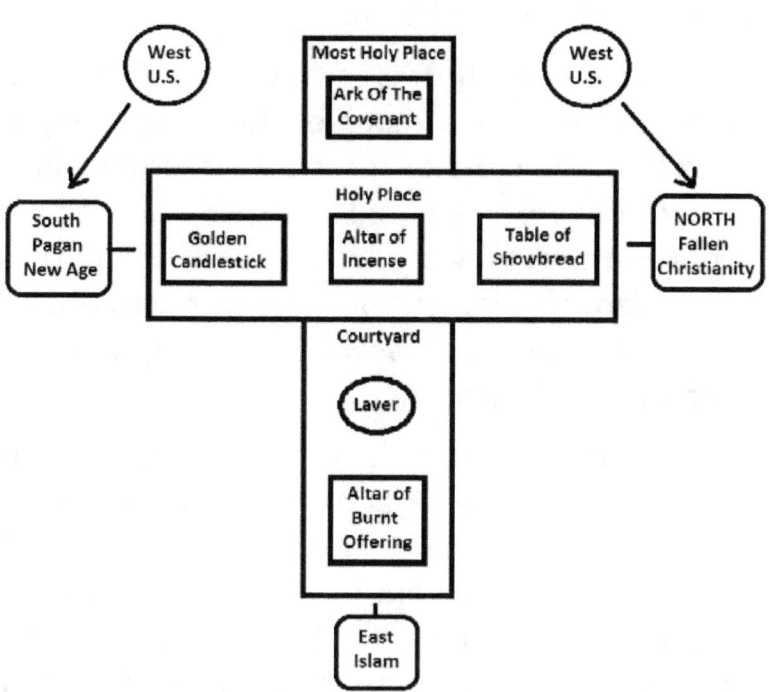

Unlike the other two fallen systems of worship, this attack that comes from the east does not attack a truth as seen in the holy place of the sanctuary. In fact, it begins in the courtyard of the sanctuary. Indeed, we find that the first lie of Satan, or point of attack through Islam, occurs at the altar of sacrifice. Before looking closer at this, let's review what we know about Islam.

Revelation 16 verse 13 states, *"And I saw three unclean spirits like frogs come out of the mouth of the dragon, and out of the mouth of the beast, and out of the mouth of the false prophet. "* We will now review these three unclean spirits as seen in the mouth of the false prophet (doctrines of Islam).

1. They deny that Christ is the true Son of God. They see him as a messenger of Allah and deny His death on the cross or resurrection for the sinner. They also are presented as having an immortal soul and thus they cannot (or surely will not) die. They deny the Father/Son relationship essentiality in their salvation as seen in the prayer of John chapter seventeen.

2. They are saved by their own works. Through pilgrimages to Mecca and other good works they teach that one becomes more enlightened by the prophets and can work to shorten time in hell or even earn Jannah (Heaven). The ultimate goal is to advance Allah's will to the entire world even by Jihad (violence and force) when necessary.

3. Once in paradise they may have all their wishes and thus have an elevated state of godlike bliss. To quote Jim Mitchell in his book "<u>Islam (The Final Chapter)</u>" on page 88 he states that in regard to heaven: **"A Muslim thinks in terms of the comforts of a refreshing oasis, circled with ready to harvest date trees, and populated with young olive eyed virgins ready for the taking."**

See how again the three original lies (unclean spirits) are again being taught by Islam. Again, notice the same three lies that were presented to Eve in the garden.

1. There is no true Son of God. Therefore there is no need for the Father/Son Spirit of God. Man will surely not die because his soul is immortal.
2. Through his own strength, enlightenment can be obtained.
3. Empowered through enlightenment, man will become like or at one with God, knowing both good and evil and enter a higher state of existence.

In this first attack as seen in the first lie we should, by now, be expecting it to be on the relationship of Jesus to the Father. Belief is not essential to have eternal life. This is exactly what Islam believes and teaches. The Koran teaches that Christ is only a prophet and a holy man. He never died for our sins but went back to heaven without dying. The first piece of furniture from the east in the sanctuary is the altar of sacrifice which is at the foot of the cross when seen overlaid on the sanctuary.

At the heart of the sanctuary doctrine is the sacrificial system representing the death of the Son of God for our sins in the death of the lamb. When John the Baptist first saw Jesus coming to the river of Jordan, he exclaimed: *"Behold the Lamb of God, which taketh away the sin of the world." (John 1:29)* Isaiah prophesied of this. *"But he was wounded for our transgressions; he was bruised* *for our iniquities: the chastisement of our peace was upon him; and with his stripes we are healed. All we like sheep have gone astray; we have turned every one to his own way; and the LORD hath laid on him the iniquity of us all. He was oppressed, and he was afflicted, yet he opened not his mouth: <u>he is brought as a lamb to the slaughter</u>, and as a sheep before her shearers is dumb, so he openeth not his mouth. He was taken from prison and from judgment: and who shall declare his generation? <u>For he was cut off out of the land of the living</u>: for the transgression of my people was he stricken.* (Isaiah 53: 5-8)

Islam teaches that even in their denial of Christ as the Son of God one may still obtain heaven or hell because everyone has an eternal soul. In this teaching is again the first lie of Satan (Jesus is not the Son of God and ye shall not surely die).

Yet Paul teaches us to: *"Let this mind be in you, which was also in Christ Jesus: Who, being in the form of God, thought it not robbery to be equal with God: But made himself of no reputation, and took upon him the form of a servant, and was made in the likeness of men: And being found in fashion as a man, he humbled himself, and became obedient unto death, even the death of the cross."* (Philippians 2:5-7) In the most beloved text in the scriptures we read that *"God so loved the world, that he gave his only begotten Son, that whosoever believeth in him should not perish, but have everlasting life."* (John 3:16) It is clearly seen in the Scriptures that there is only life eternal through belief in the gift of the Father's Son. How should we, as the remnant church, respond to this Islamic attack on the cross of Christ as seen in sanctuary?

"The Saviour has said, "He that believeth on the Son hath everlasting life: and he that believeth not the Son shall not see life; but the wrath of God abideth on him" He says again, "And this is life eternal, that they might know thee, the only true God, and Jesus Christ whom thou hast sent." <u>Mohammedanism</u> has its converts in many lands and its advocates deny the divinity of Christ. Shall this faith be propagated, and the advocates of truth fail to manifest intense zeal to overthrow the error, and teach men of the pre-existence of the only Saviour of the world? O how we need men who will search and believe the word of God, who will present Jesus to the world in his divine and human nature, declaring with power and in demonstration of the Spirit, that "there is none other name under heaven given among men, whereby we must be saved." O how we need believers who will now present Christ in life and character, who will hold him up before the world as the brightness of the Father's glory, proclaiming that God is love! <u>HM</u>, September 1, 1892 par. 4

The dying world is before you, and you can find work to do anywhere in its borders; but what are you doing for the salvation of those for whom Christ has died? God in his providence has been preparing the way for the coming of the living agent to all lands, that men may hear the good news of salvation. All things are now ready, and the angels wait for the co-operation of those who believe the truth for these last days, that they may go forth, and work with the followers of Christ in drawing souls to God.

All heaven is interested in man's salvation, and the work may be done speedily, the kingdom of God may come, and the earth be filled with the knowledge of God as the waters cover the sea. The great desire of the heavenly intelligences is that the character of God, so long misrepresented and misinterpreted, may be rightly represented before those who have been deceived by the devices of the enemy. Satan has imputed to God his own attributes, and is it not now time that the name of Christ should be great among the heathen? <u>God calls for those who have been enlightened to fall into line, and begin aggressive warfare on the strongholds of the evil one</u>." <u>HM</u>, September 1, 1892

In the second lie, Satan has Islamic believers working to obtain enlightenment through prayer rituals, pilgrimages to Mecca, and also through violence in the form of Jihad waged wars (which is simply violence against Jews, Christians, the United States, and other infidels) to force the will of Allah on the world. Christian faith, with love for your fellow man, is not a doctrine of truth in the Islamic mindset.

Missing from the doctrine of Islam is the fundamental truth that true change comes: *"Not by might, nor by power, but by my spirit, saith the LORD of hosts."* (Zechariah 4:6) Having Allah's will imposed in the world through sharia law is their goal. No great change in morality is necessary and thus you hear of those who work through terrorism to earn a heaven with 99 virgins to continually sexually serve them.

They do not accept the sacrifice of Christ in the system of the sanctuary and thus cannot be baptized into his life as seen in the laver. In their attack on the Cross, they do not seek to pervert it or deny it as the other false systems but actually seek to tear it down by attacking it at its base.

For the Muslim who accepts Christ as his personal Saviour, he must first let go of the false teachings that Allah and Yahweh are the same god. They simply cannot be. Either the Bible is wrong and full of false prophets or the Koran is wrong and thus Allah is a false prophet. They cannot both be correct. Christ Jesus either is or is not the Son of God. If He is not, the Bible is full of false prophets. If He is the Son of God, then Allah is a false prophet and his god is a different god from Yahweh. Anyone who leaves the Islamic faith is under a sentence of death according to the sharia law of Allah. According to the Bible, all who do not accept Jesus as Lord and Savior are under a sentence of death from the Father. So to the Muslim, the stakes are high.

In the sanctuary, we see that the answer can only be in accepting the sacrifice of the Lamb of God and accept that Jesus is the answer to our sin problem. It is in the acceptance of the sacrifice of Christ for our sins that the true conviction of sin occurs. Then, we must be baptized into Christ's death and resurrection as seen in the truth of the laver that lies between the altar of sacrifice and the holy place. We cannot enter the holy place from Islam without this truth.

This is where Satan's third lie is revealed. His lie fools the Islamic believer into believing that he can become like God without going through the sacrifice of Christ. *"Jesus saith unto him, I am the way, the truth, and the life: no man cometh unto the Father, but by me."* (John 14:6) **"The converting power of God can transform inherited and cultivated tendencies; for the religion of Jesus is uplifting. "Born again" means a transformation, a new birth in Christ Jesus."** AH 206

The sinner must be baptized into Christ as the living water. **""If any man thirst, let him come unto me and drink." It was the same message that had gladdened the heart of the Samaritan woman, at Jacob's well, -- "Whosoever drinketh of the water that I shall give him, shall never thirst; but the water that I shall give him, shall be in him a well of water springing up into everlasting life." Christ alone can satisfy that sense of want in the human soul. His gracious invitation reaches down even to our time. From the Fountain of life the** cry still goes forth to a lost world, "Come unto me and drink."" (RH February 28, 1882)

We cannot receive the transforming gift of God directly. Satan's promise to be like gods or to be transformed into the image of God without Jesus leads only to death. "**What promise did our Lord Jesus Christ make to His disciples to furnish them with consolation in view of His departure from them? It was the promise of the Holy Spirit of God. The divine influence of the Holy Spirit was to cooperate with the human mind and bring to their remembrance whatsoever Christ had spoken unto them. The great need of this time of peril is the Holy Spirit, for it will bring to the receiver all other blessings in its train. The truth believed will transform the character.**" CTr 371 He promised not to leave them comfortless but promised to return to them in Spirit.

As we have seen, the same three unclean spirits are in the mouths (teachings) of the dragon, the beast, and the false prophet. The attacks from the north, south, and east have each been seen. They are all directed toward the truth of the cross of Christ. They are all a propagation of the three original lies of Lucifer first told to the fallen angels, then to our deceived parents, and finally to the world in these fallen movements. They may be wrapped and packaged differently, but each reflects the heart of the arch deceiver.

"*With such a leader -- an angel expelled from heaven -- these supposedly wise men of earth may* fabricate bewitching theories with which to infatuate the minds of men. Paul said to the Galatians, "Who hath bewitched you, that ye should not obey the truth?" Satan has a masterly mind, and he has his chosen agents by which he works to exalt men, and clothe them with honor above God. But God is clothed with power; He is able to take those who are dead in trespasses and sins, and by the operation of the Spirit which raised Jesus from the dead, transform the human character, bringing back to the soul the lost image of God. Those who believe in Jesus Christ are changed from being rebels against the law of God into obedient servants and subjects of His kingdom. They are born again, regenerated, sanctified through the truth. This power of God the skeptic will not admit, and he refuses all evidence until it is brought under the domain of his finite faculties. He even dares to set aside the law of God, and prescribe the limit of Jehovah's power. But God has said, "I will destroy the wisdom of the wise, and will bring to nothing the understanding of the prudent." The Youth's Instructor, February 7, 1895

Revelations of the Cross In the Sanctuary
Part 4 - The West

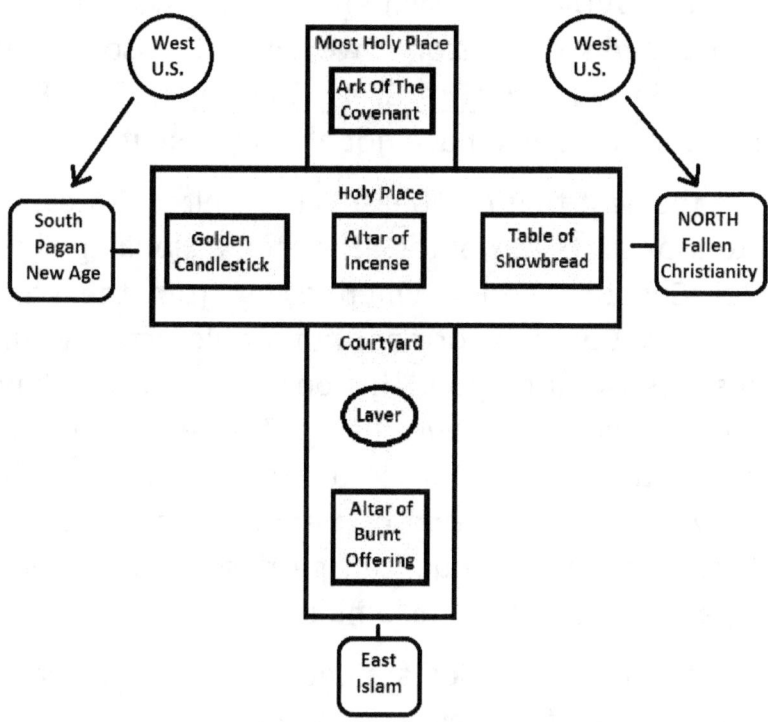

"In Revelation 13:11 John states: *"And I beheld another beast coming up out of the earth; and he had two horns like a lamb, and he spake as a dragon."* This beast did not come up out of the sea as did the other beast. The sea represents peoples or nations. This new beast represented a new beast or nation that arose around the time that the beast of Rome received its deadly wound. In history, we know that it was the United States that came into power as a new nation at this time. I will not spend much time in proving this doctrine from Scripture. There are those who have done this already. I would suggest again the <u>Total Onslaught</u> Series of DVDs by Walter Veith available at www.amazingdiscoveries.org website. I also highly recommend the book "<u>The Great Controversy</u>" by Ellen G. White for those who have not already read it.

In the light that this beast is the United States, we need to look at its attributes. It is seen as looking like a lamb or Christian nation when rising from the earth (when this nation was formed) but would actually turn out to speak like a dragon. This beast is shown to have two horns or political power bases. The political nature of the United States has turned out to exactly follow this prophecy as seen in its two primary political parties. In the Democratic and Republican parties are seen these two aspects of power or the lamb's horns.

In these two parties are seen the two aspects of our nation's beliefs. They are generally referred to as liberal and conservative. The liberal party is easily identified as tending toward paganism. The Conservative party has generally been thought to be religious in nature and thus many have felt a need to use their power to vote for this party. But the truth is that both horns (political parties) attack the truth of the cross as seen in the sanctuary.

In Revelation thirteen, verse twelve, we are told *"And he exerciseth all the power of the first beast before him, and causeth the earth and them which dwell therein to worship the first beast, whose deadly wound was healed."* Here we see that the religious arm of the United States will join hands with fallen Christianity and try to force the worship of an image set up by Rome. The Papacy has already done this in proclaiming to have changed God's second and fourth commandments. The second one they simply destroyed, but they claim to have changed the fourth one. Indeed, they say that this change of the Sabbath to Sunday is a sign or mark of their authority. Yielding to this mark of their authority is how we receive the mark of this beast.

Though many of us know this, some may not realize that when we use our power of voting, we are actually sanctioning either the power given over to the dragon power or to the beast power. Both, we have already seen, have the three unclean spirits (doctrines of devils) in their teachings. **"The Lord would have His people bury political questions. On these themes silence is eloquence. Christ calls upon His followers to come into unity on the pure gospel principles which are plainly revealed in the word of God. We cannot with safety vote for political parties; for we do not know whom we are voting for. We cannot with safety take part in any political scheme. Those who are Christians indeed will be branches of the true vine, and will bear the same fruit as the vine. They will act in harmony, in**

Christian fellowship. They will not wear political badges, but the badge of Christ. What are we to do, then?—Let political questions alone." CCh 316

Some may have a problem with this. I have even heard members of the church state that if we do not vote then we are responsible, by our silence, for the sins that occur while evil men are in office. Yet, we are shown that the opposite is true. **"We cannot with safety vote for political parties; for we do not know whom we are voting for. We cannot with safety take part in any political schemes. We cannot labor to please men who will use their influence to repress religious liberty, and to set in operation oppressive measures to lead or compel their fellow men to keep Sunday as the Sabbath. The first day of the week is not a day to be reverenced. It is a spurious sabbath, and the members of the Lord's family cannot participate with the men who exalt this day, and violate the law of God by trampling upon His Sabbath. The people of God are not to vote to place such men in office; for when they do this, they are partakers with them of the sins which they commit while in office."** FE 475

"The Lord Jesus is disappointed in his people. He is the Captain, they are to file under his banner. They have no time, wisdom, or strength to spend in taking sides with political parties. Men are being stirred with an intense activity from beneath, and the sons and daughters of God are not to give their influence to this political strife. But what kind of a spirit takes hold upon our people, when those who believe we are now under the third angel's message, the last message of mercy to the world, brothers in the same faith, appear wearing the badges of opposing political parties, proclaiming opposite sentiments and declaring their divided opinions.

Watchmen upon the walls of Zion, the people are asking you, What of the night? Can you tell them with assurance and authority, The morning cometh, and also the night? God is our Father, Christ is our Saviour. (See 2 Peter 1:16-21)

There is danger, decided danger, for all who shall link themselves up with the political parties of the world. <u>There is fraud on both sides</u>. God has not laid upon any of our people the burden of linking up with either party. We are under Christ's banner, and every one who names the name of Christ is to depart from all iniquity. Sorrow and trial will come. The faith of every one is being tested. But our Lord is truth, he is love, and his scepter stretcheth over the universe. Surprises await every one. We know not what political crisis will come next. But in regard to the political agitators, the word of the Lord to us is, "Go not ye after them." True wisdom will not lead us to follow the example of the foolish rich man of the parable. True wisdom is revealed in seeking first the kingdom of God and his righteousness." <u>GCDB</u>, February 17, 1897

The truth is that in prophecy we see that the west will not present a new doctrine but will use its political and military might to support the beast of fallen Christianity and to speak as a dragon. We can no more change this fate for our country than we could move the stars in the sky. Coming to this realization, we know that our votes will give power to the dragon or to fallen Christianity which brings on the persecution of God's saints. We must trust God in how the matters of kings and rulers will play out. Remember that Satan would seek to lie to us in this with the same three lies given to our parents.

1. We will by our votes, and not by faith in God, decide who our rulers or kings will be. Should not our king be Christ?

2. In the power of our votes, we can direct the course of our country's beliefs and spiritual path.

3. We have enough wisdom knowing both good and evil ourselves to decide the fate of an entire nation by our vote.

Remember, in chapter four we learned that: *"By me kings' reign, and princes decree justice"* (Proverbs 8:15). In John 19: 11, Jesus points this out to Pilot when He stated: *"Thou couldest have no power at all against me, except it were given thee from above"*. All kings and rulers of this world are only in power because Jesus allows them to be. Daniel told us in Daniel 2:21-22: *"Daniel answered and said, Blessed be the name of God for ever and ever: for wisdom and might are his: And he changeth the times and the seasons: he removeth kings, and setteth up kings: he giveth wisdom unto the wise, and knowledge to them that know understanding."*

I end this chapter with one final look at the cross as seen in the sanctuary. At the very center of the cross is the altar of incense. This represents where the heart of Jesus was during His sacrifice for mankind. The altar of incense shows Christ's heart tied to our prayers and mingled with His gift of love ascending up to the Father in our behalf. Here Christ intercepts fallen man and both justifies and, with the Father, sanctifies the repentant sinner.

Quoting from the Remnant Study Bible page 1568 we read: **"This altar of incense never quit burning. It was a sweet fragrance, the Bible says. Is it not a sweet thing when we know that Jesus not only forgives us but that he also continues to guide us in the right direction? He constantly says to us, "Pick up your cross, come and follow me." Do you hear him calling you?"** It is in the heart of Jesus that we are carried into the most holy place and, therefore, into the very presence of God.

"Christ might commission the angels of heaven to pour out the vials of wrath on our world, full of hypocrisy and sin, destroying those who are filled with hatred to God. He might blot this dark spot from His universe. But He does not do this. He is today standing at the altar of incense, presenting before God the prayers of those who desire His help. "Who is he that condemneth? It is Christ that died, yea rather, that is

risen again, who is even at the right hand of God, who also maketh intercession for us.'" DG 240

"Jesus knows the circumstances of every soul. You may say, I am sinful, very sinful. You may be; but the worse you are, the more you need Jesus. He turns no weeping, contrite one away. He does not tell to any all that He might reveal, but He bids every trembling soul take courage. Freely will He pardon all who come to Him for forgiveness and restoration. . . . He is today standing at the altar of incense, presenting before God the prayers of those who desire His help.

The souls that turn to Him for refuge, Jesus lifts above the accusing and the strife of tongues. No man or evil angel can impeach these souls. Christ unites them to His own divine-human nature. They stand beside the great Sin Bearer, in the light proceeding from the throne of God." CC 309

Revelations of the Cross In the Sanctuary
Part 5 - The Ark of the Covenant

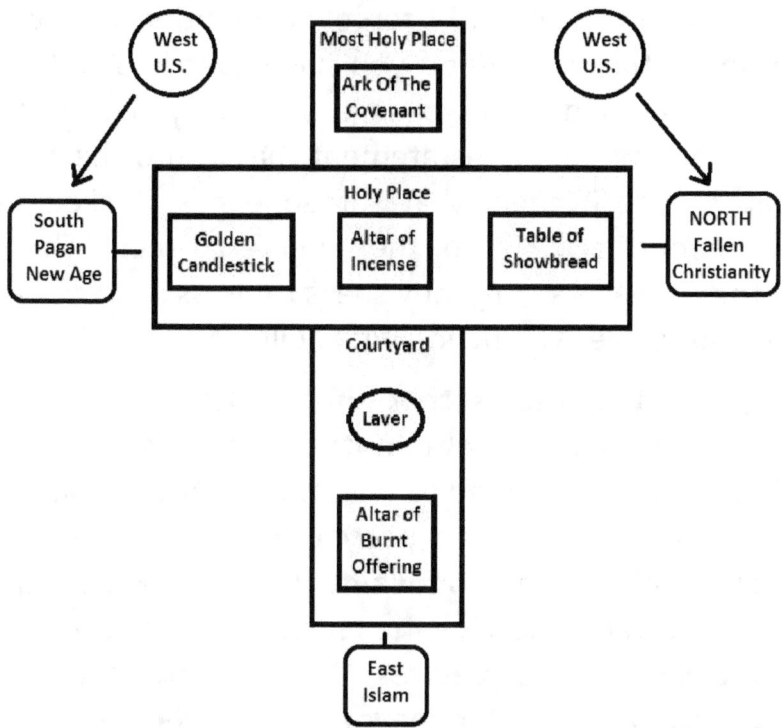

Carried by Christ behind the spiritual veil into the most holy place we have now come full circle. The repentant sinner now stands before the very God and Judge that had found him guilty of high treason in the highest court of the universe. This time, though, we do not stand alone. With us is the best attorney that all of creation has ever known. Here Christ, the very Son of God, mediates for us in our behalf. Even more remarkable is the fact that though the plea of guilty has been presented to the court, the punishment has already been paid in our behalf by this same attorney. Even more amazing is the fact that the Eternal Father and Judge has turned judgment over to our attorney. Oh, and by the way, did I forget to mention that your attorney is the best friend you have ever known? Or, that He has pledged to change your very nature and make you fit for reinstatement back into heaven's society? Does it seem that someone has stacked the odds in your favor? If so, then you're correct. That is why the deceiver so urgently seeks to press his three lies upon you to overwhelm you with guilt.

"Satan knows that those who ask God for pardon and grace will obtain it; therefore he presents their sins before them to discourage them. Against those who are trying to obey God, he is constantly seeking occasion for complaint. Even their best and most acceptable service he seeks to make appear corrupt. By countless devices, the most subtle and the most cruel, he endeavors to secure their condemnation.

In his own strength, man cannot meet the charges of the enemy. In sin-stained garments, confessing his guilt, he stands before God. But Jesus, our Advocate, presents an effectual plea in behalf of all who by repentance and faith have committed the keeping of their souls to Him. He pleads their cause, and by the mighty arguments of Calvary, vanquishes their accuser.

His perfect obedience to God's law has given Him all power in heaven and in earth, and He claims from His Father mercy and reconciliation for guilty man. To the accuser of His people He declares: "The Lord rebuke thee, O Satan. These are the purchase of My blood, brands plucked from the burning." And to those who rely on Him in faith, He gives the assurance, "Behold, I have caused thine iniquity to pass from thee, and I will clothe thee with change of raiment." (Zechariah 3:4.)

All who have put on the robe of Christ's righteousness will stand before Him as chosen and faithful and true. Satan has no power to pluck them out of the hand of the Saviour." PK 586

In the most holy place is the Ark of the Covenant. Its very name bears the wonder of God's grace. It holds the promise of escape from a condition of sin that lies beyond even our deepest hopes outside of the mercy of Christ. Its place, as seen in the cross, is where the very mind of Christ was when He was crucified and still is now in His gift for our redemption.

The cross of Jesus is the only way for man to stand before the Father being fully reconciled. All of the heavenly hosts are watching this amazing work being done on our behalf in the temple in heaven.

"In the temple in Heaven, the dwelling-place of God, his throne is established in righteousness and judgment. In the most holy place is his law, the great rule of right by which all mankind are tested. The ark that enshrines the tables of the law is covered with the mercy-seat, before which Christ pleads his blood in the sinner's behalf. Thus is represented the union of justice and mercy in the plan of human redemption. This union infinite wisdom alone could devise, and infinite power accomplish; it is a union that fills all Heaven with wonder and adoration. The cherubim of the earthly sanctuary, looking reverently down upon the mercy-seat, represent the interest with which the heavenly host contemplate the work of redemption. This is the mystery of mercy into which angels desire to look, — that God can be just while he justifies the repenting sinner, and renews his intercourse with the fallen race; that Christ could stoop to raise unnumbered multitudes from the abyss of ruin, and clothe them with the spotless garments of his own righteousness, to unite with angels who have never fallen, and to dwell forever in the presence of God." GC88 415

So in this light, claim the promise and go with Jesus into that place of rest. Accept your court appointed attorney. *"Let this mind be in you, which was also in Christ Jesus: Who, being in the form of God, thought it not robbery to be equal with God: But made himself of no reputation, and took upon him the form of a servant, and was made in the likeness of men: And being found in fashion as a man, he humbled himself, and became obedient unto death, even the death of the cross; Wherefore God also hath highly exalted him, and given him a name which is above every name: That at the name of Jesus every knee should bow, of things in heaven, and things in earth, and things under the earth; And that every tongue should confess that Jesus Christ is Lord, to the glory of God the Father ... For it is God which worketh in you both to will and to do of his good pleasure."* (Philippians 2:5-11,13)

This is but a tip of the iceberg concerning the cross of Christ and the sanctuary. It is only a dent in the surface of this deep truth. I hope this has inspired you to dig deeper. No matter how long and deep you study, there will always be more to learn.

"The cross of Christ will be the science and the song of the redeemed through all eternity. In Christ glorified they will behold Christ crucified. Never will it be forgotten that He whose power created and upheld the unnumbered worlds through the vast realms of space--the Beloved of God, the Majesty of heaven, He whom cherub and shining seraph delighted to adore-- humbled Himself to uplift fallen man; that He bore the guilt and shame of sin, and the hiding of His Father's face, till the woes of a lost world broke His heart, and crushed out His life on Calvary's cross. That the Maker of all worlds, the Arbiter of all destinies, should lay aside His glory and humiliate Himself from love to man will ever excite the wonder and adoration of the universe. As the nations of the saved look upon their Redeemer and behold the eternal glory of the Father shining in His countenance; as they behold His throne,

which is from everlasting to everlasting, and know that His kingdom is to have no end, they break forth in rapturous song: "Worthy, worthy, is the Lamb that was slain, and hath redeemed us to God, by His own most precious blood!" <u>AG</u> 98

Chapter 10
Not by Might - Nor by Power

"Not by might, nor by power, but by My Spirit, saith the Lord of hosts." (Zechariah 4:6) In this final chapter, we will put the final pieces of God's warnings and promises together as revealed by His prophets. We are truly living in the final moments of earth's history. Look at the events unfolding in the world and church. Earthquakes and natural disasters are occurring at an unprecedented rate. The Middle East is melting down as political unrest and violence threaten to consume it and the world with it. Social upheaval is spreading and threatening the United States. Within Christ's remnant church, the three fold attack is seen on the truth of the cross in the doctrines of these three unclean spirits of demons as seen in Revelation 16:13.

We know that the power and military might of the United States will soon be given to the first beast (Roman Catholicism with apostate Protestantism). It will seem like a good idea at the time. Pressure from Islam to establish sharia law through Jihad will threaten our western way of life and begin to breakdown our society. With further pressure and civil unrest coming from proponents of communism and labor/trade unions, political upheaval and civil unrest will worsen and threaten to consume the United States. The general public will feel that these events necessitate a returning to God, only this time by uniting under the banner of Rome. They will push the government to tear down the wall between church and state and establish both moral and religious laws. These will be centered on the Papal church's teachings and will include laws that violate both the second and fourth commandments of God.

"**The time is fast coming when the controlling power of the labor unions will be very oppressive.**" CL 10

"**The trades unions will be one of the agencies that will bring upon this earth a time of trouble such as has not been since the world began.**--Letter 200, 1903." CL 10.2

"In the world gigantic monopolies will be formed. Men will bind themselves together in unions that will wrap them in the folds of the enemy. A few men will combine to grasp all the means to be obtained in certain lines of business. **Trades unions will be formed, and those who refuse to join these unions will be marked men.**" Letter 26, 1903

"**Those who claim to be the children of God are in no case to bind up with the labor unions that are formed or that shall be formed. This the Lord forbids.** Cannot those who study the prophecies see and understand what is before us? Letter 201, 1902 CL 12

"O that God's people had a sense of the impending destruction of thousands of cities, now almost given to idolatry! . . .

Not long ago a very impressive scene passed before me. I saw an immense ball of fire falling among some beautiful mansions, causing their instant destruction. I heard someone say, "We knew that the judgments of God were coming upon the earth, but we did not know that they would come so soon." Others said, "You knew? Why then did you not tell us? We did not know." On every side I heard such words spoken. . .

Soon grievous troubles will arise among the nations--trouble that will not cease until Jesus comes. As never before we need to press together, serving Him who has prepared His throne in the heavens and whose kingdom ruleth over all. <u>God has not forsaken His people, and our strength lies in not forsaking Him.</u>

The judgments of God are in the land. The wars and rumors of wars, the destruction by fire and flood, say clearly that the time of trouble, which is to increase until the end, is very near at hand. We have no time to lose. The world is stirred with the spirit of war. The prophecies of the eleventh of Daniel have almost reached their final fulfillment. . . .

Last Friday morning, just before I awoke, a very impressive scene was presented before me. I seemed to awake from sleep but was not in my home. From the windows I could behold a terrible conflagration. Great balls of fire were falling upon houses, and from these balls fiery arrows were flying in every direction. It was impossible to check the fires that were kindled, and many places were being destroyed. The terror of the people was indescribable.

Strictly will the cities of the nations be dealt with, and yet they will not be visited in the extreme of God's indignation, because some souls will yet break away from the delusions of the enemy, and will repent and be converted, while the mass will be treasuring up wrath against the day of wrath." MAR 25

It is now; here in earth's final moments when the world needs us the most that Satan presses his final attack on God's remnant. Through the insidious doctrines of the trinity, pantheism and spiritualism (in the appearance of spiritual formation and contemplative prayer), and a movement to destroy God's law as a knee jerk reaction to legalism, we find our church even now in deep spiritual trouble. With the impending political pressure of enforced Sunday observance as a show of loyalty to God, it could quickly find itself appearing ready to fall.

"A train of cars was shown me, going with the speed of lightning. The angel bade me look carefully. I fixed my eyes upon the train. It seemed that the whole world was on board, that there could not be one left. Said the angel, "They are binding in bundles ready to burn." Then he showed me the conductor, who appeared like a stately, fair person, whom all the passengers looked up to and reverenced. I was perplexed and asked my attending angel who it was. He said, "It is Satan. He is the conductor in the form of an angel of light. He has taken the world captive. They are given over to strong delusions, to believe a lie, that they may be damned. This agent, the next highest in order to him, is the engineer, and other of his agents are employed in different offices as he may need them, and they are all going with lightning speed to perdition." EW 88.2

The truth concerning these false doctrines will by nature be divisive and the church's response collectively will shake God's beloved bride to her foundations. With these false doctrines in place, the church will feel increased with doctrinal goods and in need of nothing. Yet, there will be those who shine light on the straight testimony (given by God through Ellen White) called forth by the counsel of the True Witness to the Laodiceans. Each member must face these truths and choose either to follow the traditions of men or accept God's reproof and correction. We must not be consumed by the enemy within, just as we are standing on the borders of heavenly Canaan, but stand firm in the truth and warn the church and the world.

Yet, there is one more aspect of this attack on the church we must look at. We are shown that victory will not be by power (self-empowerment) or might (self-enlightenment) but by God's Spirit (not our deified spirit).

The great truth of the Spirit of God is the key to our relationship to Christ and thus our salvation. Remember that other than us individually, there is no one else in the most holy place except the Father and the Son. We also have seen that in the counsel of the Father no other being could enter except Christ. In John chapter fourteen Jesus stated that He had to leave them so that God would send Him (the Spirit of truth) back to them spiritually. This Holy Spirit, we are told, would be sent from the Father in Christ's name and that through it He would manifest Himself to them. Further on He stated that He would not leave them comfortless. He would come to them. He stated that the world would not know this Spirit but that they would because He was dwelling with them and would be in them.

"*If ye love me, keep my commandments. And I will pray the Father, and he shall give you another Comforter, that he may abide with you for ever; Even the Spirit of truth; whom the world cannot receive, because it seeth him not, neither knoweth him: but ye know him; for he dwelleth with you, and shall be in you. I will not leave you comfortless: I will come to you. Yet a little while, and the world seeth me no more; but ye see me: because I live, ye shall live also. <u>At that day ye shall know that I am in my Father, and ye in me, and I in you.</u> [21] He that hath my commandments, and keepeth them, he it is that loveth me: and he that loveth me shall be loved of my Father, and I will love him, and will manifest myself to him. Judas saith unto him, not Iscariot, Lord, how is it that thou wilt manifest thyself unto us, and not unto the world? Jesus answered and said unto him, <u>If a man love me, he will keep my words: and my Father will love him,</u>*

and we will come unto him, and make our abode with him." (John 14:15-23)

Here we are told that the Spirit of God is the presence of the Father and Son in the heart and mind of their true disciples. Indeed, we see that this truth is key in not falling to the last great apostasy that threatens to rock our church and bring on the shaking. Let's examine the evidence for this truth.

"Be not deceived; many will depart from the faith, giving heed to seducing spirits and doctrines of devils. We have now before us the alpha of this danger. The omega will be of a most startling nature. We need to study the words that Christ uttered in the prayer that He offered just before His trial and crucifixion." 1SM 197

In this prayer, Jesus reveals that it is the combined work of Himself and His Father that would protect us from falling to this deception, and that it would be their working together that sanctifies the church. *"Neither pray I for these alone, but for them also which shall believe on me through their word; That they all may be one; as thou, Father, art in me, and I in thee, that they also may be one in us: that the world may believe that thou hast sent me. And the glory which thou gavest me I have given them; that they may be one, even as we are one: I in them, and thou in me, that they may be made perfect in one; and that the world may know that thou hast sent me, and hast loved them, as thou hast loved me."* (John 17:20-23)

"True sanctification comes through the working out of the principle of love. God is love; and he that dwelleth in love dwelleth in God and God in him." 1John 4:16. The life of him in whose heart Christ abides will reveal practical godliness. The character will be purified, elevated, ennobled, and glorified. Pure doctrine will blend with works of righteousness; heavenly precepts will mingle with holy practices. AA 560

This relationship to God and Jesus, as seen in their Spirit's relationship to us as a church, is likened unto a marriage. *"Husbands, love your wives, just as Christ also loved the church and gave Himself for her, that He might <u>sanctify and cleanse</u> her with the washing of water by the word, that He might present her to Himself a glorious church, not having spot or wrinkle or any such thing, but that she should be holy and without blemish."* (Ephesians 5:25-27)

Time after time we are told that it is the Father bringing Jesus into our lives that sanctifies us. This working together is the same work often described as the work of the Spirit of God or the Holy Spirit. John said that we would know in that day that it is the Father and Son who would make their abode within us. *"That good thing which was committed to you, keep by the Holy Spirit who dwells in us."* (2 Timothy 1:14) *"Therefore let that abide in you which you heard from the beginning. If what you heard from the beginning abides in you, you also will abide in the Son and in the Father."* (1 John 2:24)

We also see in Ephesians 5:25-27 that it is their combined presence that sanctifies us. **"...all the workers are to blend in harmony, controlled by the sanctifying influence of the Holy Spirit."** AA 275 **"The Spirit of God should have perfect control of us, influencing us in all our actions. If we have a right hold on Heaven, a right hold of the power that is from above, we shall feel the sanctifying influence of the Spirit of God upon our hearts."** CH 45

The prophet identifies the same job of sanctification as being done by the Spirit of God. Another job of the Holy Spirit is to bring us to knowledge of truth. In the prayer of the prophet below, we see that spiritual eye salve comes from the Father.

"My heavenly Father, we come to Thee at this time as children dependent upon Thee. We are weakness itself. In us there is no strength, no comeliness. But we come to Thee as Thy little children. We want special help from Thee at this time. Thou hast promised in Thy word that Thou wilt sanctify those who keep Thy Sabbath. We want the sanctification of the Holy Spirit upon our hearts, upon our characters. O my Father, for Christ's sake wilt Thou pardon our transgressions and our sins. Wilt Thou give us clear spiritual eyesight, that we may discern what we should be, and what we must be, if we are granted entrance

into the kingdom of God, if we hear the words, "Well done, thou good and faithful servant." GCB, April 6, 1903

In their working together, the Father and Son bring us into the truth of Jesus and what He did on the cross. Here, through manifesting His Son to us, the Father's love is revealed. Any other teaching would be removing Christ from our hearts and thus in the broad sense would be an antichrist doctrine. *"Who is a liar but he who denies that Jesus is the Christ? He is antichrist who denies the Father and the Son."* (1John 2:22)

"The Spirit is given as a regenerating agency, to make effectual the salvation wrought by the death of our Redeemer. The Spirit is constantly seeking to draw the attention of men to the great offering that was made on the cross of Calvary, to unfold to the world the love of God, and to open to the convicted soul the precious things of the Scriptures." AA 52

How do we get this regenerating agency in our lives? Note the use of the word "agency". An agency by its very name is a plural of agents who work together. *"And this is eternal life, that they may know You, the only true God, and Jesus Christ whom You have sent."* (John 17:3) *"for it is God who works in you both to will and to do for His good pleasure."* (Philippians 2:13) Jesus said: *"I am the way, the truth, and the life. No one comes to the Father except through Me"* (John 14:6)

Here is the beautiful truth. Only the Father can bring Christ into your life and only Christ can present you to the Father. Thus in the Father's great love for mankind in giving up His Son to die on the cross, He made Christ the means by which He could again live in our hearts. Likewise Christ, demonstrating His great love for us, became the mediator to present us back to the Father. It's the perfect agency of salvation and redemption for mankind. *"For there is one God and one Mediator between God and men, the Man Christ Jesus."* (1Timothy 2:5)

Thus we are brought back into fellowship with them both. *"That which was from the beginning, which we have heard, which we have seen with our eyes, which we have looked upon, and our hands have handled, concerning the Word of life - the life was manifested, and we have seen, and bear witness, and declare to you that eternal life which was with the Father and was manifested to us - that which we have seen and heard we declare to you, that you also may have fellowship with us; and <u>truly our fellowship is with the Father and with His Son Jesus Christ</u>."* (1John 1:1-3) In 2 Corinthians 13:14, we see this fellowship with the Father and the Son being called fellowship with their Spirit. *"The grace of the Lord Jesus Christ, and the love of God, and the communion of the Holy Spirit be with you all. Amen."*

This truth was often seen in the beginning of letters sent by Paul to different churches and their leaders in the New Testament. *"To Timothy, a true son in the faith: Grace, mercy, and peace from God our Father and Jesus Christ our Lord."* (1Timothy 1:2) "To Titus, a true son in *our* common faith: Grace, mercy, *and* peace from God the Father and the Lord Jesus Christ our Savior." (Titus 1:4) The apostle John also expressed this in his letters *"Grace, mercy, and peace will be with you from God the Father and from the Lord Jesus Christ, the Son of the Father, in truth and love."* (2John 1:3)

"In His prayer to the Father, Christ gave to the world a lesson which should be graven on mind and soul. "This is life eternal," He said, "that they might know Thee the only true God, and Jesus Christ, whom Thou hast sent." John 17:3. This is true education. It imparts power. <u>The experimental knowledge of God and of Jesus Christ whom He has sent, transforms man into the image of God</u>." COL 114

Here is where it gets sticky for some people. Since this fellowship is with an agency of the Father and Son, it will often, if not always, be the combined work of both. Thus if we try to define what the Holy Spirit is, as it works in our lives, we can come up with wrong ideas or conceptions. That is why we are cautioned not to try. The Father is the omnipotent, omnipresent Ancient of Days. We simply cannot fathom all of His workings.

"The Father cannot be described by the things of earth. <u>The Father is all the fullness of the Godhead bodily, and is invisible to mortal sight.</u> We must not attempt to lift with presumptuous hand the curtain

behind which He veils His majesty. The apostle exclaims: "How unsearchable are his judgments, and his ways past finding out!" Romans 11:33. It is a proof of His mercy that there is the hiding of His power, that He is enshrouded in the awful clouds of mystery and obscurity; for to lift the curtain that conceals the divine presence is death. No mortal mind can penetrate the secrecy in which the Mighty One dwells and works. We can comprehend no more of His dealings with us and the motives that actuate Him than He sees fit to reveal. He orders everything in righteousness, and we are not to be dissatisfied and distrustful, but to bow in reverent submission. He will reveal to us as much of His purposes as it is for our good to know; and beyond that we must trust the hand that is omnipotent, the heart that is full of love." FLB 39

How can we understand a God that can be everywhere at once and be in communication with all beings at once? That is why we are told that the Spirit would not speak of Himself.

"Holiness is not rapture: it is an entire surrender of the will to God; it is living by every word that proceeds from the mouth of God; it is doing the will of our heavenly Father; it is trusting God in trial, in darkness as well as in the light; it is walking by faith and not by sight; it is relying on God with unquestioning confidence, and resting in His love. It is not essential for us to be able to define just what the Holy Spirit is. Christ tells us that the Spirit is the

Comforter, "the Spirit of truth, which proceedeth from the Father." It is plainly declared regarding the Holy Spirit that, in His work of guiding men into all truth, "**He shall not speak of Himself**. John 15:26; 16:13" AA 51. Christ said in John 14 that it would manifest Him.

Here is where we, as a people, have not followed God's instructions as revealed by His prophet. By adopting a trinity doctrine, in an attempt to not appear as a cult to the world, we have proceeded and done the very thing we were advised not to do. We have tried to make the Spirit speak of itself. This is what happens when we do not listen to the testimonies given to us as a people. Concerning the Holy Spirit, we have tried to identify it in relationship to the Father and Son. We placed this human only effort in a book, Seventh-day Adventists Believe, which claims to represent the doctrines of our faith. Yet, we are told the following:

"The nature of the Holy Spirit is a mystery. Men cannot explain it, because the Lord has not revealed it to them. Men having fanciful views may bring together passages of Scripture and put a human construction on them, but the acceptance of these views will not strengthen the church. Regarding such mysteries, which are too deep for human understanding, silence is golden.

The office of the Holy Spirit is distinctly specified in the words of Christ: "When He is come, He will reprove the world of sin, and of righteousness, and of judgment." John 16:8. It is the Holy Spirit that

convicts of sin. If the sinner responds to the quickening influence of the Spirit, he will be brought to repentance and aroused to the importance of obeying the divine requirements." AA 52

All we can truly know of the Holy Spirit is that it proceeds from the Father and that it brings the Father and Son into the heart of the believer. This book is not trying to define what the Holy Spirit is. We are clearly told that we have not been given this. What we are clearly shown is that through it the Son of God is brought into the heart of the believer. Through it, the Father is brought back into reconciliation with man by Christ Jesus. We should have been more concerned with receiving it and less determined to define it.

We got into trouble when we tried to use our own wisdom in coming up with a handbook of beliefs instead of using the Bible and the Bible alone as our creed of faith. **"When God's word is studied, comprehended, and obeyed, a bright light will be reflected to the world; new truths, received and acted upon, will bind us in strong bonds to Jesus. The Bible, and the Bible alone, is to be our creed, the sole bond of union; all who bow to this holy word will be in harmony. Our own views and ideas must not control our efforts. Man is fallible, but God's word is infallible. Instead of wrangling with one another, let men exalt the Lord. Let us meet all opposition as did our Master, saying, "It is written." Let us lift up the banner on which is inscribed,**

The Bible our rule of faith and discipline." <u>The Review and Herald</u>, Dec. 15, 1885

"Though the Reformation gave the Scriptures to all, yet the selfsame principle which was maintained by Rome prevents multitudes in Protestant churches from searching the Bible for themselves. They are taught to accept its teachings as interpreted by the church; and there are thousands who dare receive nothing, however plainly revealed in Scripture, that is contrary to their creed or the established teaching of their church.

Notwithstanding the Bible is full of warnings against false teachers, many are ready thus to commit the keeping of their souls to the clergy. There are today thousands of professors of religion who can give no other reason for points of faith which they hold than that they were so instructed by their religious leaders. They pass by the Saviour's teachings almost unnoticed, and place implicit confidence in the words of the ministers. But are ministers infallible? How can we trust our souls to their guidance unless we know from God's word that they are light bearers?" <u>GC</u> 597

This is by no means an attack on our leaders or clergy. We all allowed this. We are all equally responsible and answerable to God. Whether actively participating or sitting by quietly not studying God's word for ourselves, we all allowed the enemy to infiltrate us with doctrines that our founding church fathers rejected and are in total conflict with the God given pillars of faith upon which this church was founded.

"Let the truths that are the foundation of our faith be kept before the people. Some will depart from the faith, giving heed to seducing spirits and doctrines of devils. They talk science, and the enemy comes in and gives them an abundance of science; but it is not the science of salvation. It is not the science of humility, of consecration, or of the sanctification of the Spirit. **We are now to understand what the pillars of our faith are,--the truths that have made us as a people what we are, leading us on step by step.** Review and Herald, May 25, 1905

"Landmarks of Truth, Experience, and Duty.-- **Messages of every order and kind have been urged upon Seventh-day Adventists, to take the place of the truth which, point by point, has been sought out by prayerful study, and testified to by the miracle-working power of the Lord. But the waymarks which have made us what we are, are to be preserved, and they will be preserved, as God has signified through His word and the testimony of His Spirit.** He calls upon us to hold firmly, with the grip of faith, to the fundamental principles that are based upon unquestionable authority." Special Testimonies, Series B, No. 2, p. 59

"**As a people we are to stand firm on the platform of eternal truth that has withstood test and trial. We are to hold to the sure pillars of our faith. The principles of truth that God has revealed to us are our** only true foundation. **They have made us what we are. The lapse of time had not lessened their value**." Special Testimonies, Series B, No. 2, p. 51, 1904

"**No line of truth that has made the Seventh-day Adventist people what they are, is to be weakened. We have the old landmarks of truth, experience, and duty, and we are to stand firmly in defense of our principles, in full view of the world**." (Testimonies, Vol. 6, p. 17)

"In the future, deception of every kind is to arise, and we want solid ground for our feet. We want solid pillars for the building. **Not one pin is to be removed from that which the Lord has established.** The enemy will bring in false theories, such as the doctrine that there is no sanctuary. This is one of the points on which there will be a departing from the faith. **Where shall we find safety unless it be in the truths that the Lord has been giving for the last fifty years?**" Review and Herald, May 25, 1905

Remember that this last statement was written in 1905. The last 50 years she spoke of was a time when our forefathers firmly established this church as non-trinitarian, firmly opposing spiritualism and mystic doctrines, resolutely defending God's law of love, and presenting the three angel's messages with power to the world.

So one might ask at this point what the summation of this book is. It is that we as humanity must confess that we joined in that great rebellion and were guilty of high treason against God, His Son, and His great law of love. It is that God, in demonstrating His love, rescued us and paid our debt with His dearest blood and made it possible for us to be reinstated back into heaven's society. This is the good news of the Gospel. The Father and the Son together have worked out our salvation and made it available to the entire world.

It is in this radiance that God raised up the remnant church to take this Gospel in the light of the third angel's message to this dark and dying planet. Satan realizes that his doom is at hand and in his last ditch effort of malice and hatred has made war on God's remnant people, who keep the commandments of God and have the testimony of Jesus.

His battle strategy has not changed. In this final remnant church, he has attacked the position and relationship of the Son, the nature of His Father, and the truth concerning His law. As we have seen, this has been done through the multigenerational change from non-trinitarianism to trinitariansism, the continued assault of pantheism as seen in the introduction of spiritualism through spiritual formation and contemplative prayer, and the attack on the Father's law in relation to righteousness by faith in Christ's merits alone. What is needed is for God's chosen people to recognize the danger, sound the alarms from the walls of Zion and to return to the primitive godliness once delivered to His saints.

"Before the final visitation of God's judgments upon the earth, there will be, among the people of the Lord, such a revival of primitive godliness as has not been witnessed since apostolic times. The Spirit and power of God will be poured out upon His children. At that time many will separate themselves from those churches in which the love of this world has supplanted love for God and His word. Many, both of ministers and people, will gladly accept those great truths which God has caused to be proclaimed at this time, to prepare a people for the Lord's second coming. The enemy of souls desires to hinder this work; and before the time for such a movement shall come, he will endeavor to prevent it, by introducing a counterfeit. In those churches which he can bring under his deceptive power, he will make it appear that God's special blessing is poured out; there will be manifest what is thought to be great religious interest. . . .

"Wherever men neglect the testimony of the Bible, turning away from those plain, soul-testing truths which require self-denial and renunciation of the world, there we may be sure that God's blessing is not bestowed. . . . A wrong conception of the character, the perpetuity, and the obligation of the divine law, has led to errors in relation to conversion and sanctification, and has resulted in lowering the standard of piety in the church. Here is to be found the secret of the lack of

the Spirit and power of God in the revivals of our time . . . It is only as the law of God is restored to its rightful position that there can be a revival of primitive faith and godliness among His professed people. "Thus saith the Lord, Stand ye in the ways, and see, and ask for the old paths, where is the good way, and walk therein, and ye shall find rest for your souls." Jeremiah 6:16."
FLB 326

There is, even now, a solemn awakening occurring within God's church as we see His Spirit slowly being withdrawn from the world. This revival is not like the counterfeits that have come in the past. It is not a revival of pomp and emotion. There is no fanciful sensation driven feelings of love, joy, celebration, and hype motivated jubilation. Instead, there is seen a people who, with deep soul searching and a profound conversion of the heart and soul, are being led by God's quickening truth and inward abiding presence of His Spirit. With this is an awakened, earnest desire to reach out to the misguided souls still languishing in misery and lost in the darkness of Babylon with the light of God's immeasurable love as reflected in His people.

Soon the bridegroom will approach and the call will go out, "go ye out and meet Him". My brothers and sisters, now is the time to receive the oil of God's Spirit while it may yet be found.

"Time is almost finished. Do you reflect the lovely image of Jesus as you should?" Then I was pointed to the earth and saw that there would have to

be a getting ready among those who have of late embraced the third angel's message. Said the angel, "Get ready, get ready, get ready. Ye will have to die a greater death to the world than ye have ever yet died." I saw that there was a great work to do for them and but little time in which to do it." EW 64.1

It is my solemn hope and prayer: **"That He would grant you, according to the riches of His glory, to be strengthened with might by His Spirit in the inner man; that Christ may dwell in your hearts by faith; that ye, being rooted and grounded in love, may be able to comprehend with all saints what is the breadth, and length, and depth, and height; and to know the love of Christ, which passeth knowledge, that ye might be filled with all the fulness of God."** BEcho, Nov 20, 1899

The great conflict is nearly over. Soon we will be in that glorious home where sin, death and sorrow will be no more. Seeing this home God's messenger wrote, **"And the years of eternity, as they roll, will bring richer and still more glorious revelations of God and of Christ. As knowledge is progressive, so will love, reverence, and happiness increase. The more men learn of God, the greater will be their admiration of his character. As Jesus opens before them the riches of redemption, and the amazing achievements in the great controversy with Satan, the hearts of the ransomed thrill with more fervent devotion, and with more rapturous joy they sweep the harps of gold; and ten thousand times ten** thousand and thousands of thousands of voices unite to swell the mighty chorus of praise.

"And every creature which is in Heaven, and on the earth, and under the earth, and such as are in the sea, and all that are in them, heard I saying, Blessing, and honor, and glory, and power, be unto Him that sitteth upon the throne, and unto the Lamb forever and ever." [Revelation 5:13.]

The great controversy is ended. Sin and sinners are no more. The entire universe is clean. One pulse of harmony and gladness beats through the vast creation. From Him who created all, flow life and light and gladness, throughout the realms of illimitable space. From the minutest atom to the greatest world, all things, animate and inanimate, in their unshadowed beauty and perfect joy, declare that God is love." GC88 678

"He which testifieth these things saith, Surely I come quickly. Amen. Even so, come, Lord Jesus. The grace of our Lord Jesus Christ be with you all. Amen." (Revelation 22:20-21)

Below is list of references that include abbreviations used in this book. References that were complete in the text are not included in this list. Also please note that in quoting from these and other works (as well as the Scriptures) that underlining and emphasis provided is often my own.

REF	Title	Author
1MR	Manuscript Releases Volume One	Ellen G White
1SM	Selected Messages Vol. 1	Ellen G White
4T	Testimonies for the Church Vol. 4	Ellen G White
AA	Acts of the Apostles	Ellen G White
AG	God's Amazing Grace	Ellen G White
AH	The Adventist Home (1952)	Ellen G White
CC	Conflict and Courage	Ellen G White
CCH	Counsels for the Church	Ellen G White
CH	Counsels on Health	Ellen G White
CET	Christian Experience and Teachings	Ellen G White
CL	Country Living	Ellen G White
COL	Christ's Object Lessons	Ellen G White
CR -	Christ and His Righteousness	E.J. Waggoner
CSA	A Call To Stand Apart	Ellen G White
CTr	Christ Triumphant	Ellen G White
DA -	Desire of Ages	Ellen G White
DG	Daughters of God	Ellen G White
DS	The Day-Star	Ellen G White
EV	Evangelism	Ellen G White
EW	Early Writings	Ellen G White
FE	Fundamentals of Christian Education	Ellen G White
FLB	The Faith I Live By	Ellen G White
GC	The Great Controversy	Ellen G White
GC88	The Great Controversy (1888)	Ellen G White
GCB	The General Conference Bulletin	Ellen G White
GCDB	General Conference Daily Bulletin	Ellen G White
HM	The Home Missionary	Ellen G White
LDE	Last Day Events	Ellen G White
MAR	Maranatha (1976)	Ellen G White
PK	Prophets and Kings	Ellen G White
PP -	Patriachs and Prophets	Ellen G White
RH	The Review and Herald	Ellen G White
TDG	This Day With God	Ellen G White
BEcho	The Bible Echo	Ellen G White
SpTA 12	Special Testimonies Series A	Ellen G White

www.ingramcontent.com/pod-product-compliance
Lightning Source LLC
LaVergne TN
LVHW051549070426
835507LV00021B/2493